LAW STUDENT PROFESSIONAL DEVELOPMENT
AND FORMATION

Law schools currently do an excellent job of helping students to "think like a lawyer," but empirical data show that clients, legal employers, and the legal system need students to develop a wider range of competencies. This book helps legal educators to understand these competencies and provides practical ways to build them into a law school curriculum. Based on recommendations from the American Bar Association, the American Association of Law Schools, and the Carnegie Foundation for the Advancement of Teaching, it will equip students with the skills they need not only to think but also to act and feel like a lawyer. With this proposed model, students will internalize the need for professional development toward excellence, their responsibility to others, a client-centered approach to problem solving, and strong well-being practices. These four goals constitute a lawyer's professional identity, and this book empowers legal educators to foster each student's development of a professional identity that leads to a gratifying career that serves society well. This title is Open Access.

Neil W. Hamilton has focused on the professional development and formation of law students in his teaching since 1987 and in his scholarship since 2001 with fifty-seven law journal articles and a book, ROADMAP: *The Law Student's Guide to Meaningful Employment* (2d ed. 2018). He is the Thomas and Patricia Holloran Professor of Law and founding director of the Holloran Center for Ethical Leadership in the Professions at the University of St. Thomas School of Law.

Louis D. Bilionis is Dean Emeritus and Droege Professor of Law at the University of Cincinnati College of Law and a Fellow at the Holloran Center. An experienced administrator, teacher, and scholar, he has focused particularly on strategies for leading change in legal education.

Law Student Professional Development and Formation

BRIDGING LAW SCHOOL, STUDENT, AND EMPLOYER GOALS

NEIL W. HAMILTON

University of St. Thomas

LOUIS D. BILIONIS

University of Cincinnati

CAMBRIDGE
UNIVERSITY PRESS

CAMBRIDGE
UNIVERSITY PRESS

University Printing House, Cambridge CB2 8BS, United Kingdom

One Liberty Plaza, 20th Floor, New York, NY 10006, USA

477 Williamstown Road, Port Melbourne, VIC 3207, Australia

314–321, 3rd Floor, Plot 3, Splendor Forum, Jasola District Centre,
New Delhi – 110025, India

103 Penang Road, #05–06/07, Visioncrest Commercial, Singapore 238467

Cambridge University Press is part of the University of Cambridge.

It furthers the University's mission by disseminating knowledge in the pursuit of
education, learning, and research at the highest international levels of excellence.

www.cambridge.org
Information on this title: www.cambridge.org/9781108745659
DOI: 10.1017/9781108776325

© Cambridge University Press 2022

First published 2022

A catalogue record for this publication is available from the British Library.

Library of Congress Cataloging-in-Publication Data
NAMES: Hamilton, Neil W., author. | Bilionis, Louis D., author.
TITLE: Law student professional development and formation : bridging law school, student, and
employer goals / Neil W. Hamilton, University of St. Thomas; Louis D. Bilionis, University of
Cincinnati.
DESCRIPTION: Cambridge, United Kingdom ; New York, NY : Cambridge University Press, 2022. |
Includes bibliographical references and index.
IDENTIFIERS: LCCN 2021062709 (print) | LCCN 2021062710 (ebook) | ISBN 9781108745659 (paper-
back) | ISBN 9781108776325 (ebook)
SUBJECTS: LCSH: Practice of law – Study and teaching – United States.
CLASSIFICATION: LCC KF272 .H36 2022 (print) | LCC KF272 (ebook) | DDC 340.071/173–dc23/eng/
20220208
LC record available at https://lccn.loc.gov/2021062709
LC ebook record available at https://lccn.loc.gov/2021062710

ISBN 978-1-108-74565-9 Paperback

To my children and their spouses, Shaan and Laura, Maya and Derek, and Kyra and Jon, who inspire me each day through their tireless love and support of the next generations. – NWH

To the mentors who have known me better than I know myself – my wife Ann Hubbard, our daughter Graciela, Judith Wegner, Martha Crunkleton, and John Williams. – LDB

Contents

Figures

Tables

Acknowledgments

Our students for the seventy-seven years that we jointly have been teaching law have inspired us and helped us to grow each year. We are deeply grateful. We write this book in the hope that we can pay forward to future generations of law students all that we have been given by our students and by those who mentored and coached us over the years. Our hope is that law schools will help all law students to visualize and achieve their goals while living toward widening circles of care and service to others and the values of our profession.

We deeply appreciate all the support we have received over many years from both of our law schools, the University of St. Thomas School of Law and the University of Cincinnati College of Law, and our colleagues at both schools. Lest there be any doubt, we are not speaking for our schools in this book.

We stand on the shoulders of many people in writing this book and to them we are also deeply grateful. Tom Holloran played an enormous role in shaping this book. Tom is the model of the lawyer we hope our students become, our mentor and friend, and the visionary and benefactor who in 2006 created the Thomas Holloran Center for Ethical Leadership in the Professions, which has supported our work leading to this book. Jerry Organ, a founding faculty member at St. Thomas with Professor Hamilton in 2001 who joined the Holloran Center in 2009 and became its codirector in 2016, has shaped our ideas, encouraged us, and partnered in growing the center. Center Fellows Barbara Glesner-Fines, Dean at UMKC School of Law, and Professor Kendall Kerew at Georgia State have also provided important creative support and encouragement.

There are so many wonderful colleagues nationally, sailing under different flags, with whom we have communed and shared ideas and support and who have inspired us. There are too many to list individually here, but they include more than 250 faculty and staff from more than 40 law schools who have been participants in the Holloran Center summer workshops on law student professional formation. We are also very grateful to all the scholars whose work we cite in this book.

Earlier work by leaders in the field whose work has been particularly influential for us include Bill Sullivan, Ann Colby, Judith Wegner, Lloyd Bond, and Lee Shulman, the authors of *Educating Lawyers* in 2007. Drs. Eric Holmboe and Robert Englander have generously shared the experience of medical schools with competency-based education.

The Holloran Center coordinator, Brady King, provided key support on all of the tables and figures. Annie Boeckers, a rising third-year student at the University of St. Thomas, gave us valuable support on the footnotes.

Writing a book is like running a marathon but stretched out over several years. We are grateful most of all for our spouses, Uve Hamilton and Ann Hubbard, for getting us through all the challenges with ideas, support, editing help, and love throughout. They are the wing-people who are always alongside us in life.

Introduction

The Four Foundational Professional Development and Formation (PD&F) Goals and Their Benefits for Students, Faculty, Staff, and Administrators

Do you believe that "thinking like a lawyer" is an important professional skill, but by no means all that there is to being a lawyer? Do you think that being a professional calls for the development of a wide range of competencies? Do you seek to understand those competencies better? Do you think that being a professional should involve the exploration of the values, guiding principles, and well-being practices foundational to successful legal practice?[1] Are you interested in new and effective ways to build these competencies, values, and guiding principles into a law school's curriculum? Would you like a framework for improving your own law school's attention to these competencies, guiding principles, and values along with practical suggestions you can consider? Would you like to help better prepare students for gratifying careers that serve society well?

This book is written for law school faculty, staff, and administrators who would like to see their school more effectively help each student to understand, accept, and internalize the following:

1. Ownership of continuous professional development toward excellence at the major competencies that clients, employers, and the legal system need;

2. a deep responsibility and service orientation to others, especially the client;

---

[1] At its February 2022 meeting, the ABA House of Delegates approved revisions to Standard 303 that require each law school "to provide substantial opportunities to students for: ... the development of a professional identity." Newly adopted Interpretation 303-5 defines "professional identity" as an exploration of "what it means to be a lawyer and the special obligations lawyers have to their clients and society. The development of professional identity should involve an intentional exploration of the values, guiding principles, and well-being practices considered foundational to successful legal practice." https://www.americanbar.org/content/dam/aba/images/news/2022/02/midyear-hod-resolutions/300.pdf.

3. a client-centered problem-solving approach and good judgment that
   ground each student's responsibility and service to the client; and
4. well-being practices.

These four goals taken together state what it means for an individual to think,
act, and feel like a lawyer. They constitute a lawyer's professional identity.
They also define the foundational learning outcomes[2] of the professional
development and formation of law students movement in legal education in
the United States.[3] They figure centrally in all that follows in this book. We

---

[2]   "Learning outcomes" are defined as "clear and concise statements of knowledge that the
     students are expected to acquire, skills students are expected to develop, and values that they
     are expected to understand and integrate into their professional lives. The outcomes should
     identify the desired knowledge, skills, and values that a school believes that its students should
     master." Managing Director's Guidance Memo, Standards 301, 302, 314, and 315 (June 2015) at
     page 4. www.americanbar.org/content/dam/aba/administrative/legal_education_and_
     admissions_to_the_bar/governancedocuments/2015_learning_outcomes_guidance.authcheck
     dam.pdf. Standards 314 and 315 require that a learning outcome must be measurable using
     formative, summative, and program assessment. *Id.* at 4–5.
[3]   The first three goals are the most common elements of the formation of a professional identity
     in all five of the Carnegie Foundation for the Advancement of Teaching's studies of education
     for the clergy (2007), lawyers (2007), engineers (2009), nurses (2010), and physicians (2010)
     based on many dozens of site visits at schools in each profession. *See* Neil Hamilton, *Fostering
     Professional Formation (Professionalism): Lessons from the Carnegie Foundation's Five Studies
     of Educating Professionals,* 45 CREIGHTON L. REV. 763, 765, 775 (2012). All five Carnegie
     studies emphasize that the most fundamental element of the formation of a professional
     identity is internalizing responsibility to the person being served (e.g., parishioner, client,
     patient). Four of the studies agree on two other foundational goals: (1) a commitment to growth
     toward excellence at all the competencies needed for the profession and (2) good judgment/
     moral reasoning in the context of the interpersonal relationship with the person served. *Id.* at
     775–76. Hamilton's empirical study of lawyer professionalism award winners in Minnesota also
     found a common understanding among them that their professional formation and develop-
     ment included (1) a deep responsibility to others, especially deep care for the client that builds
     trust; (2) ongoing reflection and career-long learning; and (3) counseling the client with candid
     and honest counsel and independent judgment. *See* Neil Hamilton & Verna Monson, *Ethical
     Professional Transformation: Themes from Interviews About Professionalism with Exemplary
     Lawyers,* 52 SANTA CLARA L. REV. 921, 948–49, 957 (2012). The fourth goal reflects recent
     major concerns of law schools and the profession. The Carnegie study of legal education was
     published in 2007. *See* WILLIAM M. SULLIVAN, ET AL., EDUCATING LAWYERS:
     PREPARATION FOR THE PROFESSION OF LAW (2007) [hereinafter EDUCATING LAWYERS].
     In the years since the publication of *Educating Lawyers,* and particularly in the past several
     years, there has been much greater awareness that the well-being of law students and lawyers is
     profoundly important to the legal profession and to the clients that lawyers serve. Illuminating
     sources on that development include Jerome M. Organ, David B. Jaffe & Katherine
     M. Bender, *Suffering in Silence: The Survey of Law Student Well-Being and the Reluctance
     of Law Students to Seek Help for Substance Use and Mental Health Concerns,* 66 J. LEGAL
     EDUC. 116, 116–56 (Autumn 2016), (discussing the 2014 Survey of Law Student Well Being),
     and NAT'L TASK FORCE ON LAWYER WELL-BEING, *The Path to Lawyer Well-Being:
     Practical Recommendations for Positive Change* (2017) [hereinafter *Path to Lawyer*

will speak of them as the four foundational professional development and formation goals – or, for convenience and brevity, the four "PD&F" goals.

If any of these goals are important to you, this book explains how to help your students achieve them. Importantly, this book also explains how you can influence others – the faculty, staff, and administrators at your school; your students; and the legal employers your graduates serve – to adopt these goals and take steps to achieve them. We look first at the benefits from a more effective curriculum on each of the four goals.

1.1 THE BENEFITS OF A MORE EFFECTIVE CURRICULUM TO FOSTER PD&F GOAL 1: EACH STUDENT'S OWNERSHIP OF CONTINUOUS PROFESSIONAL DEVELOPMENT TOWARD EXCELLENCE AT THE COMPETENCIES THAT CLIENTS, LEGAL EMPLOYERS, AND THE LEGAL SYSTEM NEED

Law students, faculty, staff, and administrators want to increase the probabilities of better academic performance, bar passage, and meaningful postgraduation employment for each student. Strong empirical data show that student growth toward later stages of ownership of continuous professional development (as reflected in self-directed/self-regulated learning) enhances student academic performance,[4] and that stronger student academic performance in turn correlates with higher probabilities of bar passage.[5] Diversity,

---

Well-Being], https://www.americanbar.org/content/dam/aba/images/abanews/ThePathToLaw yerWellBeingReportRevFINAL.pdf.

[4] "Research has amassed overwhelming evidence that self-regulated learning enhances student performance and achievement in courses and course units." LINDA NILSON, CREATING SELF-REGULATED LEARNERS 10–11 (2013). "It has been shown that self-regulated learning is one of the best predictors of academic performance" and "self-regulated learners are more effective learners." Susanna Lucieer et al., *Self-regulated Learning and Academic Performance in Medical Education*, 38 MED. TEACH. 585, 586 (2016). Self-regulated activity "has consistently been found to be related to student achievement." Renee Jansen et al., *Self-Regulated Learning Partially Mediates the Effect of Self-Regulated Learning Interventions on Achievement in Higher Education: A Meta-Analysis*, 28 EDUC. RESEARCH REV. 1, 2 (2019). "Students who were willing to reflect and make changes in their learning strategies and who selected active strategies that inherently involved regulating their learning were more likely to have academic success." Jennifer Gundlach & Jessica Santangelo, *Teaching and Assessing Metacognition in Law School*, 69 J. LEGAL EDUC. 156, 180 (2019).

[5] See LINDA F. WIGHTMAN, LAW SCH. ADMISSION COUNSEL, LSAC NATIONAL LONGITUDINAL BAR PASSAGE STUDY 37 (1998); Douglas Rush & Hisako Matsuo, *Does Law School Curriculum Affect Bar Examination Passage? An Empirical Analysis of Factors Related to Bar Examination Passage During the Years 2001 Through 2006 at a Midwestern Law School*, 57 J. LEGAL EDUC. 224, 232–33 (2007); Katherine A. Austin, Catherine Martin Christopher & Darby Dickerson, *Will I Pass the Bar Exam? Predicting Student Success Using LSAT Scores and Law School Performance*, 45 HOFSTRA L. REV. 253, 266–68 (2017).

equity, inclusion, and belonging initiatives aimed at helping disadvantaged students[6] also benefit substantially from a more effective curriculum (particularly a continuous coaching model of the kind we will analyze in Chapter 4) that fosters belonging and provides institutional support to navigate the educational environment and the job market.[7]

To the extent that online learning may provide lower levels of support and guidance to students than in-person classroom education, self-directed/self-regulated learning skills characterized by student skill in planning, managing, and controlling their learning processes become even more important for student performance.[8] Data also show that legal employers and clients greatly value initiative and ownership of continuous professional development;[9] a student who can communicate evidence of later-stage development on self-directed/self-regulated learning will demonstrate strong value to potential employers.

1.2 THE BENEFITS OF A MORE EFFECTIVE CURRICULUM TO FOSTER PD&F GOAL 2: EACH STUDENT'S DEEP RESPONSIBILITY AND SERVICE ORIENTATION TO OTHERS, ESPECIALLY THE CLIENT

Many law faculty and staff would like to see each law graduate internalize a deep responsibility and service orientation to others, particularly the client. We also know that a substantial proportion of undergraduate students in the applicant pool are seeking a career with opportunities to be helpful to others and useful to society.[10]

---

[6] Disadvantaged groups in law school are groups whose members are historically underrepresented in the legal profession due to their backgrounds. Dorainne Green et al., *Group-Based Inequalities in Relationship Quality are Associated with Disparities in Belonging, Satisfaction, and Achievement in Law School*, forthcoming at J. OF EDUC. PSYCH., at 12.

[7] An increased sense of belonging is linked to increased academic motivation, engagement, intention to persist, and achievement. *See* Elizabeth Bodamer, *Do I Belong at This Law School: How Perceived Experiences of Bias, Stereotype Concerns, and Social Capital Influence Law Students' Sense of Belonging* (dissertation submitted to Indiana University Graduate School, Dec. 2020) at 3, 35–36 (https://www.stthomas.edu/hollorancenter/). The more that minoritized students experience social support and social capital in the law school, the greater their sense of belonging. *Id.* at 6, 8, 39–41, 148, 151.

[8] Rene Kizilcec et al., *Self-Regulated Learning Strategies Predict Learner Behavior and Goal Attainment in Massive Open Online Courses*, 104 COMPUTERS & EDUC. 18–33 (Jan. 2017).

[9] NEIL W. HAMILTON, ROADMAP: THE LAW STUDENT'S GUIDE TO MEANINGFUL EMPLOYMENT 18–34 (2d ed. 2018) [hereinafter ROADMAP].

[10] See the discussion *infra* of what applicants to law school want in Chapter 5, Section 5.8.1.

Deep care for the client is the principal foundation for client trust in both the individual lawyer and the profession itself.[11] That deep care essentially entails a fiduciary disposition or fiduciary mindset, using "fiduciary" in the general meaning of founded on trustworthiness.[12] Each law student and new lawyer must learn to internalize a responsibility to put the client's interests before the lawyer's self-interest.[13] As Professor Greg Sisk emphasizes in a recent treatise on legal ethics: "When the lawyer protects confidential information and exercises loyal and independent judgment uninfected by conflicting interests or the lawyer's own self-interest, the lawyer's responsibilities are distinctly fiduciary in nature. In these matters, the trust of the client is directly at stake."[14]

The legal profession also holds out other fiduciary mindset values and guiding principles relating to trust in each lawyer. For example, the Preamble of the Model Rules of Professional Conduct states, "[a] lawyer should strive to attain the highest level of skill, to improve the law and the legal profession, and to exemplify the legal profession's ideals of public service."[15] It declares, "a lawyer should seek improvement of the law, access to the legal system, the administration of justice and the quality of the service rendered by the legal profession" and emphasizes the following:

> A lawyer should be mindful of deficiencies in the administration of justice and of the fact that the poor, and sometimes persons who are not poor, cannot afford adequate legal assistance. Therefore, all lawyers should devote professional time and resources and use civic influence to ensure equal access to our system of justice for all those who because of economic or social barriers cannot afford or secure adequate legal counsel.[16]

The Model Rules contemplate that a lawyer will possess very broad discretion when exercising professional judgment to fulfill responsibilities to clients, the legal system, and the quality of justice – and that the lawyer also has

---

[11] William M. Sullivan, *Foreword* to TEACHING MEDICAL PROFESSIONALISM: SUPPORTING THE DEVELOPMENT OF A PROFESSIONAL IDENTITY ix, xi, xv (Richard L. Cruess et al. eds., 2d ed. 2016).

[12] *See id.* at ix; William Sullivan, *Align Preparation with Practice*, 85 N.Y. ST. B. A. J. No. 7, 41–43 (Sept. 2013) (where Sullivan introduces the concept of fiduciary disposition).

[13] Law school accreditation standards reflect this requirement. Standard 302(c) provides: "A law school shall establish learning outcomes that shall, at a minimum, include competency in the following: (c) Exercise of proper professional and ethical responsibilities to clients and the legal system." *Standard 302(c), 2021–2022 Standards and Rules of Procedure for Approval of Law Schools*, A.B.A. SECTION OF LEGAL EDUC. & ADMISSIONS TO THE BAR.

[14] GREG SISK ET AL. LEGAL ETHICS, PROFESSIONAL RESPONSIBILITY, AND THE LEGAL PROFESSION 295 (2018).

[15] A.B.A. MODEL RULES OF PROF'L CONDUCT Preamble para. 7 (2020).

[16] *Id.*, para. 6 (2020).

a personal interest in being an ethical person who makes a satisfactory living. The Preamble recognizes that "difficult ethical issues" can arise from these potentially conflicting responsibilities and interests. "Within the framework of these Rules," the Preamble observes, "many difficult issues of professional discretion can arise. Such issues must be resolved through the exercise of *sensitive professional and moral judgment* guided by the basic principles underlying the Rules."[17] As the Preamble further notes, "a lawyer is also guided by personal conscience and the approbation of professional peers."[18]

The Model Rules recognize that clients also face many difficult ethical issues, and a lawyer should provide "*independent professional judgment* and render candid advice" to help the client think through decisions that affect others.[19] As the comments to Rule 2.1 note, "[a]dvice couched in narrow legal terms may be of little value to a client, especially where practical considerations, such as cost or effects on other people, are predominant . . . . It is proper for a lawyer to refer to the relevant moral and ethical considerations in giving advice."[20] The lawyer is not imposing the lawyer's morality on the client; rather, the "relevant moral and ethical considerations" upon which the lawyer is to draw and offer counsel – and therefore needs to comprehend – include the client's own tradition of responsibility to others.

The foregoing implicitly defines the elements of a law student's and lawyer's fiduciary mindset. They call on each law student and lawyer to

1. Comply with the *ethics of duty* – the minimum standards of competency and ethical conduct set forth in the Rules of Professional Conduct;

2. foster in oneself and other lawyers the *ethics of aspiration* – the core values and guiding principles of the profession, including putting the client's interests first;

3. develop and be guided by personal conscience – including the exercise of "sensitive professional and moral judgment" and the conduct of an "ethical person"– when deciding all the "difficult issues of professional discretion" that arise in the practice of law;

4. develop independent professional judgment, including moral and ethical considerations, to help the client think through decisions that affect others; and

5. promote a justice system that provides equal access and eliminates bias, discrimination, and racism.

[17] *Id.*, para. 9 (2020) (emphasis added).
[18] *Id.*, para. 8 (2020).
[19] *Id.*, R. 2.1 (2020) (emphasis added).
[20] *Id.*, R. 2.1 cmt. 2 (2020).

Fostering each student's development toward later stages of responsibility, service, and care for the client and the legal system has obvious benefits for students. As we discuss in Chapter 5, principle 8, research shows that students rank service to others as a significant personal objective that motivates them to pursue a career in law.[21] Supporting students in this way also contributes to the missions of many law schools and the aspirations of many faculty and staff, advancing the ideals and core values of the profession including service to the disadvantaged. As we shall see in the next section, benefits flow to clients and legal employers as well. They value client-centered lawyering and creative problem solving in the lawyer's exercise of good independent professional judgment emphasized by the Model Rules.

1.3 THE BENEFITS OF A MORE EFFECTIVE CURRICULUM TO FOSTER PD&F GOAL 3: EACH STUDENT'S CLIENT-CENTERED PROBLEM-SOLVING APPROACH AND GOOD INDEPENDENT PROFESSIONAL JUDGMENT THAT GROUND EACH STUDENT'S RESPONSIBILITY AND SERVICE TO THE CLIENT

Legal employers and clients want law graduates who demonstrate deep responsibility and service orientation to others, ownership over continuous professional development toward excellence, a client-centered problem-solving approach, and good independent professional judgment. Law students (prospective new lawyers) who have evidence of later-stage development of these competencies can increase their probability of meaningful employment – a major benefit to the students and their law school as well.

A growing number of empirical studies are defining the capacities and skills that clients and legal employers need in their changing markets, reaching results that substantially converge in support of the central importance of the third PD&F goal. Among the major studies are the following:

1. The 2003 Shultz/Zedeck survey, including principally University of California–Berkeley alumni, identifying lawyer effectiveness factors;[22]
2. Hamilton's 2012–14 and 2017 surveys of the competencies assessed by large firms, small firms, state attorneys general offices, county attorneys offices, and legal aid offices;[23]

---

[21] See the discussion *infra* at Chapter 5, Section 5.8.1.

[22] Marjorie Shultz & Sheldon Zedeck, *Predicting Lawyer Effectiveness: Broadening the Basis for Law School Admissions Decisions*, 36 LAW & SOC. INQUIRY 620, 629 (2011).

[23] *See* ROADMAP, *supra* note 9, at 24–33.

3. The Institute for the Advancement of the American Legal System 2016 study of 24,137 lawyers' responses to the question of what competencies are "necessary in the short term" for law graduates;[24]

4. Thomson Reuters' 2018–19 interviews and survey of law-firm professional development lawyers and hiring managers on what are the most important competencies for a successful twenty-first-century lawyer;[25]

5. The Institute for the Advancement of the American Legal System 2019 study on the competencies that clients want, based on a random sample of 2,232 AVVO client reviews of lawyers in the period 2007–17;[26]

6. The 2019 Association of Corporate Counsel survey of 1,639 respondents who self-identified as the highest-ranking lawyer in a company;[27]

7. The 2019 BTI Consulting Group's Client Service A-Team Survey of Law Firm Client Service Performance, which includes data from 350 in-depth telephone interviews with senior in-house counsel at large organizations;[28]

8. The 2020 National Conference of Bar Examiners survey of 3,153 newly licensed lawyers (up to three years of practice) and 11,693 not recently licensed lawyers asking how frequently newly licensed lawyers performed specifically listed tasks;[29]

9. The 2020 Institute for the Advancement of the American Legal System's national study using fifty focus groups, asking respondents about the knowledge and skills that new lawyers used during the first year of practice;[30]

---

[24] *See* Alli Gerkman & Logan Cornett, Foundations for Practice: The Whole Lawyer and the Character Quotient (2016), https://iaals.du.edu/sites/default/files/documents/publications/foundations_for_practice_whole_lawyer_character_quotient.pdf.

[25] Natalie Runyon, *Delta Model Update: The Most Important Area of Lawyer Competency – Personal Effectiveness Skills*, Thomson Reuters (Mar. 21, 2019), http://www.legalexecutiveinstitute.com/delta-model-personal-effectiveness-skills/. Thomson Reuters followed up with a questionnaire survey of a broader group of practitioners on the client side. *See* Natalie Runyon & Alyson Carrel, Adapting for 21st Century Success: the Delta Lawyer Competency Model (2019), https://legal.thomsonreuters.com/content/dam/ewp-m/documents/legal/en/pdf/white-papers/delta-lawyer-competency.pdf.

[26] Logan Cornett, Think Like a Client (2019), https://iaals.du.edu/sites/default/files/documents/publications/think_like_a_client.pdf.

[27] Ass'n Corp. Couns., 2019 ACC Chief Legal Officers Survey (2019), https://www.acc.com/sites/default/files/resources/upload/2019-ACC-Chief-Legal-Officers-Survey.pdf.

[28] Bti Consulting Group, Bti Client Service A-Team 2019: Survey of Law Firm Client Service Performance (2019), https://bticonsulting.com/themadclientist/bti-client-service-a-team-2019-survey-of-law-firm-client-service-performance.

[29] Nat'l Conf. Bar Examiners Testing Task Force, Phase 2 Report: 2019 Practice Analysis (2020).

[30] Deborah Jones Merritt & Logan Cornett, Building a Better Bar: The Twelve Building Blocks of Minimum Competence 14 (2020). The study had 200 total participants with 41 focus groups of junior lawyers who had been licensed between January 1, 2016, and January 31, 2019, and had worked at least 12 months in one or more positions that required a law

10. Lisa Rohrer and Mitt Regan's in-depth interviews with 278 law partners at larger US law firms to assess whether business concerns are eclipsing professional values in law firm practice, published in 2021;[31] and

11. The National Association for Law Placement report on a 2020 Survey of Law Firm Competency Expectations for Associate Development published in 2021 based on survey results from fifty large-firm competency models.[32]

The work of leading futurists looking at the legal services market reinforces the picture. They emphasize that the competencies needed for a successful twenty-first-century lawyer include a more proactive entrepreneurial mindset to meet changing market conditions for clients and lawyers alike.[33]

All of the aforementioned studies essentially asked lawyers and clients to identify the most important competencies needed to practice law. While both attorneys and clients include client-service orientation and relationship skills among the important competencies needed to represent clients, the clients emphasize these skills more heavily (including communication, attentive listening, responsiveness, understanding of the client's context and business, and explanation of fee arrangements).[34]

Synthesizing all these empirical studies into a useful model of the foundational competencies that clients and legal employers need can be a challenge. In a recent white paper, Thomson Reuters presents what it has titled the "Delta" model of lawyer competency. The model groups lawyer competencies into three categories, with each category represented by one of the three sides of a triangular figure. The base of the triangle represents the technical skills traditionally associated with lawyering. The upper two sides of the triangle represent "personal effectiveness factors" and "business and operations" competencies, respectively.[35] We find much to favor in the Delta model; its chosen visual form for depicting the differing

---

license. Also included were nine focus groups of experienced lawyers who had supervised at least one junior lawyer during the two years preceding the study.

[31] Mitt Regan & Lisa H. Rohrer, Big Law: Money and Meaning in the Modern Law Firm 2 (2020).

[32] Nat'l Ass'n L. Placement, Report on 2020 Survey of Law Firm Competency Expectations for Associate Development (2021), https://www.nalp.org/uploads/NALP_Associate_Competencies_Report_May_2021.pdf.

[33] See, e.g., Jordan Furlong, Law Is A Buyer's Market: Building A Client-First Law Firm 29, 73–81, 145–52 (2017); Richard Susskind, Tomorrow's Lawyers: An Introduction to Your Future 4–14 (2013); William Henderson, *Efficiency Engines: How Managed Services Are Building Systems for Corporate Legal Work*, ABA J. 38–45 (June 2017).

[34] Randall Kiser, Soft Skills for the Effective Lawyer 2–33 (2017).

[35] See Delta Lawyer Competency Model, *supra* note 25, at 5.

yet interrelated competencies of effective lawyering strikes us as particularly effective. A model that serves the needs of legal educators does well to draw from the Delta model, but it needs important adaptations to reflect insights about professional education, the student's formation of professional identity, and methods of competency-based education – and also to incorporate the fuller range of competencies identified by the aforementioned studies.

Building on the Delta model approach, we offer here a Foundational Competencies Model (depicted in Figure 1) that law school faculty, staff, and administrators can consider and modify to best articulate the competencies that clients and legal employers served by their school's graduates need. Appendix A provides a summary of the empirical studies mentioned earlier that also can be useful to inform faculty and staff discussion. The model in Figure 1 reflects four principles that should inform any model developed for an individual law school:

1. The model should be based on the best available current data on the competencies that clients and legal employers need;
2. the model should be clear and understandable to a new law student and include a manageable number of competencies;
3. the model should be in the language that legal employers use, thereby helping students communicate their value to employers; and
4. the model's foundational competencies should be translatable directly into institutional learning outcomes established by the law school.

The empirical studies also support the conclusion that the following six traditional technical competencies that law schools emphasize are necessary but not sufficient to meet client and legal employer needs in changing markets:

1. Knowledge of doctrinal law in the basic subject areas;
2. legal analysis;
3. legal research;
4. written and oral communication in the legal context;
5. legal judgment; and
6. knowledge of the law-of-lawyering responsibilities to clients and the legal system.[36]

---

[36]　These are the competencies listed in the ABA's accreditation standards. *See Standards 302 (a)-(c), 2021-2022 Standards and Rules of Procedure for Approval of Law Schools*, A.B.A. SECTION OF LEGAL EDUC. & ADMISSIONS TO THE BAR.

The additional competencies that the studies indicate clients and legal employers need from lawyers in changing markets include the following:

1. Superior client focus and responsiveness to the client;
2. exceptional understanding of the client's context and business;
3. effective communication skills, including listening and knowing your audience;
4. creative problem-solving and good professional judgment in applying all of the previously noted competencies;
5. ownership over continuous professional development (taking initiative) of both the traditional technical competencies previously listed, the client relationship competencies previously listed, and the skills or habits described later;
6. teamwork and collaboration;
7. strong work ethic;
8. conscientiousness and attention to detail;
9. grit and resilience;
10. organization and management of legal work (project management); and
11. an entrepreneurial mindset to serve clients more effectively and efficiently in changing markets.

Figure 1 visually represents a Foundational Competencies Model that captures and conceptually organizes all these major competencies that clients and legal employers need. At the center of the Foundational Competencies Model – visually and conceptually – is each student's internalization of a deep responsibility and service orientation to others, especially the client, that creates trust. That internalized commitment informs all the other competencies. The center of the model also includes well-being practices because lawyers must care for themselves to care for others.

The center of the Foundational Competencies Model could also include a deep responsibility and service orientation to the legal system itself in terms of a commitment to improve the legal system and pro bono service for the disadvantaged. These internalized commitments are not emphasized in the empirical data on the capacities and skills that clients and legal employers want, but the law faculty and the legal profession may emphasize these commitments.

The bottom side of the model makes clear that each student and lawyer must demonstrate the basic technical legal competencies that clients and employers need. The left side of the model makes clear the foundational importance to clients and employers of each student and new lawyer demonstrating client-centered problem solving and good professional judgment in serving the client – including superior client focus and responsiveness,

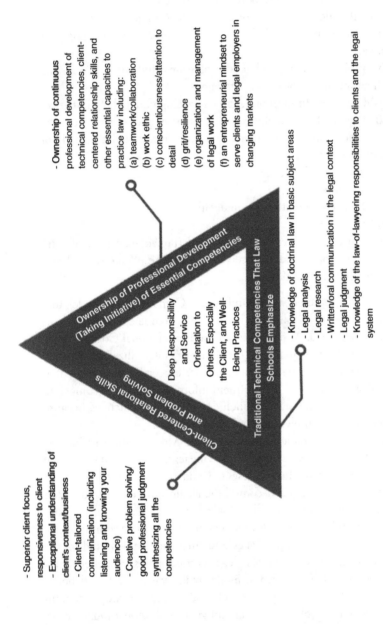

- Ownership of continuous professional development of technical competencies, client-centered relationship skills, and other essential capacities to practice law including:
  (a) teamwork/collaboration
  (b) work ethic
  (c) conscientiousness/attention to detail
  (d) grit/resilience
  (e) organization and management of legal work
  (f) an entrepreneurial mindset to serve clients and legal employers in changing markets

Ownership of Professional Development (Taking Initiative) of Essential Competencies

Deep Responsibility and Service Orientation to Others, Especially the Client, and Well-Being Practices

Client-Centered Relational Skills and Problem Solving

Traditional Technical Competencies That Law Schools Emphasize

- Knowledge of doctrinal law in basic subject areas
- Legal analysis
- Legal research
- Written/oral communication in the legal context
- Legal judgment
- Knowledge of the law-of-lawyering responsibilities to clients and the legal system

- Superior client focus, responsiveness to client
- Exceptional understanding of client's context/business
- Client-tailored communication (including listening and knowing your audience)
- Creative problem solving/good professional judgment synthesizing all the competencies

These traditional competencies reflect ABA Accreditation Standard 302(a)–(c).

FIGURE 1 Foundational Competencies Model based on empirical studies of the competencies clients and legal employers need

exceptional understanding of the client's context and business, and communication skills including listening and knowing the audience.[37] The right side of the model makes clear the foundational importance for clients and employers of ownership of continuous professional development (taking initiative) toward excellence at the competencies needed, harnessed to an entrepreneurial mindset to serve well in rapidly changing markets for both employers and clients. Employers and clients need strong teamwork and collaboration skills, a strong work ethic, conscientiousness and attention to detail, grit and resilience, and organization and management of legal work. An entrepreneurial mindset includes constant attention to client goals and completion of work more effectively and efficiently, including making effective use of technology.

A student or new lawyer who demonstrates later-stage development of these foundational competencies will benefit clients and legal employers and has a higher probability of meaningful postgraduation employment and long-term success in a service profession like law. These outcomes benefit the student, while also benefitting the law school and its faculty, staff, and administration. The law school also can demonstrate to enrolled students – and prospective applicants – that it is helping them achieve their goals of bar passage and meaningful postgraduation employment.

1.4 THE BENEFITS OF A MORE EFFECTIVE CURRICULUM TO FOSTER PD&F GOAL 4: STUDENT WELL-BEING PRACTICES

In response to increasing evidence of chronic stress, anxiety, depression, and addictive behaviors among law students and lawyers,[38] many law faculty and staff have heightened their concern about student well-being. Lawrence Krieger and Kennon Sheldon analyze a robust branch of modern positive psychology – self-determination theory (SDT) – that provides an empirical framework to understand student well-being. It also outlines the benefits to students, faculty, and staff of increasing student well-being.

What is well-being? Krieger and Sheldon treat subjective well-being in their studies as the sum of (1) life satisfaction and (2) positive affect or mood (after subtracting negative affect). They utilize established instruments on each factor. Life satisfaction includes a personal (subjective) evaluation of objective circumstances such as one's work, home, relationships, possessions, income,

---

[37] Note that in the early years of practice for a new lawyer in a firm or law department, the "client" is essentially the experienced lawyer giving the new lawyer work.

[38] *See* PATH TO LAWYER WELL-BEING, *supra* note 3, at 7.

and leisure opportunities. Positive and negative affects are purely subjective, straightforward experiences of "feeling good" or "feeling bad."[39]

What are the basic psychological needs that contribute to student well-being? Self-determination theory defines three basic psychological needs contributing to well-being: (1) autonomy (to feel in control of one's own goals and behaviors), (2) competence (to feel one has the needed skills to be successful), and (3) relatedness (to experience a sense of belonging or attachment to other people).[40] Note that the first two professional development and formation goals with which we began this chapter (ownership of continuous professional development toward excellence and a deep responsibility and service orientation to others, especially the client) reflect significant aspects of SDT's three basic psychological needs.

Autonomy is considered the most important of the three basic psychological needs since people must have a well-defined sense of self and express their core values in daily life to function in a consistent way.[41] SDT posits that there are positive outcomes for subordinates when organizational authorities support their autonomy by giving them (1) as much choice as possible, (2) a meaningful rationale to explain decisions, and (3) a sense that authorities are aware of and care about their point of view.[42] These positive outcomes include (1) higher self-determined career motivation, (2) higher well-being, and (3) higher academic performance.[43]

Sheldon and Krieger's three-year longitudinal study of students with very similar LSAT scores and undergraduate grade point averages at two law

---

[39] Lawrence S. Krieger & Kennon M. Sheldon, *What Makes Lawyers Happy? A Data-Driven Prescription to Redefine Professional Success*, 83 GEO. WASH. L. REV. 554, 564, 582–85 (2015).

[40] *See* Lawrence Krieger, *The Most Ethical of People, the Least Ethical of People: Proposing Self-Determination Theory to Measure Professional Character Formation*, 8 U. ST. THOMAS L. J. 168, 171–72 (2011). Self-determination theory also identifies four intrinsic values that mirror the three basic psychological needs and lead to behaviors that fulfill the three basic needs and thus promote well-being. The four intrinsic values are (1) self-understanding and growth (the importance of learning and personal growth), (2) intimacy with others (the importance of trusting close relationships with others), (3) helping others (improving others' lives, especially those in need), and (4) being in and building community (improving society).

[41] *See id.*

[42] Kennon M. Sheldon & Lawrence S. Krieger, *Understanding the Negative Effects of Legal Education on Law Students: A Longitudinal Test of Self-Determination Theory*, 33 PERSONALITY AND SOCIAL PSYCH. BULL. No. 6, 883, 884 (June 2007).

[43] *Id.* at 885.

schools compared student outcomes at the law school where students perceived stronger autonomy support with outcomes at the law school where students perceived weaker autonomy support. Students at the school with stronger autonomy support had higher well-being, better academic performance on grades, more self-determined motivation to pursue their legal careers, and better performance on the bar examination.[44] Krieger and Sheldon followed up with surveys submitted from 7,865 practicing lawyers in four states.[45] The responses from practicing lawyers affirmed that autonomy, competence, and relatedness strongly predict respondents' well-being.[46] The practicing lawyers also affirmed that autonomy support from supervisors increased their well-being and self-determined motivation.[47]

In Chapter 4, we will outline how law schools can utilize coaching to provide autonomy support and help improve well-being for each student. In addition to helping students achieve their goals, faculty and staff who provide that support will help the school to achieve its goals of improved bar passage and postgraduation employment outcomes.

1.5 REALIZING THESE BENEFITS AT YOUR SCHOOL

The next two chapters focus on strategic planning to realize the foregoing benefits at your school. Chapter 2 explains and stresses the importance of purposefulness in the law school's efforts to help students to realize the four PD&F goals. The reader will find a framework for bringing that purposefulness to work in the law school. Chapter 3 explores how competency-based education can serve as a possible framework for purposeful support of students toward the four goals. That discussion will introduce the reader to important lessons that legal education can learn from the experience of medical education, which changed its accreditation requirements to require competency-based education fifteen years earlier than legal education.

Chapters 4 and 5 focus on practical implementation steps to realize the benefits we just outlined at your law school. Chapter 4 brings forward ten principles from the literature on higher education that should inform the development of any law school curriculum to foster each student's progressive growth toward later stages of development on the four PD&F

---

[44] *Id.* at 893–94.
[45] The 7,865 lawyers who responded constituted a 12.7 percent response rate to the surveys sent out. Krieger & Sheldon, *supra* note 39 at 570.
[46] *Id.* at 583, 617.
[47] *Id.* at 583, 618.

goals. Chapter 5 stays with the practical, turning attention to how inter-ested faculty, staff, and administrators can lead their school toward more purposeful support of students and their PD&F goals. Recognizing that the various, and sometimes differing, interests of the major stakeholders of a law school influence the school's actions, Chapter 5 presses the importance of a clear understanding of those interests. That understand-ing, we believe, can only be obtained by going where each major stakeholder actually is, and we illustrate how to do that. The good news is that stakeholder interests *can* converge on a shared interest in student progress toward the four PD&F goals. As Chapter 5 explains, bridges can be built to connect stakeholders and their interests to the law student's realization of PD&F goals.

A Summary of the Empirical Studies That Define the Foundational Competencies That Clients and Legal Employers Need[1]

This summary can be used to inform faculty and staff discussion of the data on the competencies that graduates need to serve clients and legal employers well. The law school's learning outcomes should reflect these needs.

In *ROADMAP: The Law Student's Guide to Meaningful Employment*,[2] Neil Hamilton observed substantial convergence among (1) the 2003 Shultz/ Zedeck survey of University of California–Berkeley alumni identifying lawyer effectiveness factors;[3] (2) the author's 2012 to 2014 and 2017 surveys of the competencies assessed by large firms, small firms, state attorneys general offices, county attorneys offices, and legal aid offices;[4] and (3) the Institute for the Advancement of American Legal Studies 2016 study of 24,137 lawyers' responses to the question of what competencies are "necessary in the short term" for law graduates.[5] All of these studies essentially asked lawyers to identify the most important competencies needed to practice law. Table 1 shows the convergence of these empirical studies up to 2018 (when the second edition of the ROADMAP was published) on the competencies that clients and legal employers want beyond the basic technical legal skills.

There are more recent empirical studies of the clients' desired competencies to compare with the previous competencies identified by the lawyer respondents. First, in 2018, Thomson Reuters interviewed thirteen practitioners including both buyers of legal services and law firm talent development professionals (the study does not report how many of each) asking the following question: What are the top ten competencies that are

---

[1] The material in Tables 1–6 first appeared in Neil Hamilton, *The Gap Between the Foundational Competencies Clients and Legal Employers Need and the Learning Outcomes Law Schools Are Adopting*, 89 UMKC L. Rev. 559 (2021).

[2] Neil W. Hamilton, ROADMAP: The Law Student's Guide to Meaningful Employment 24–33 (2d ed. 2018) [hereinafter ROADMAP].

[3] Marjorie Shultz & Sheldon Zedeck, *Predicting Lawyer Effectiveness: Broadening the Basis for Law School Admissions Decisions*, 36 L. & Soc. Inquiry 620, 629 (2011).

[4] ROADMAP, *supra* note 2, at 2–33.

[5] Alli Gerkman & Logan Cornett, Foundations for Practice: The Whole Lawyer and the Character Quotient 4, 29 (2016), https://iaals.du.edu/sites/default/fil es/documents/publications/foundations_for_practice_whole_lawyer_character_quotient.pdf.

TABLE 1 *Convergence of the empirical studies on the nontechnical competencies that lawyers and legal employers identify as important for the practice of law*[6]

Ownership of Continuous Proactive Professional Development Over a Career
• Commitment to professional development toward excellence, including habit of actively seeking feedback and reflection • Initiative/strong work ethic/diligence, plus project management that demonstrates these

Internalization of Deep Responsibilities to Others (the client, the team, the employing organization, the legal system)
• Trustworthiness and integrity • Relationship skills, including respect for others, understanding of and responsiveness to client, and listening • Good judgment/common sense • Teamwork and collaboration

important for a successful twenty-first century lawyer?[7] Table 2 indicates the results of the initial Thomson Reuters interviews.

Asking the same question, Thomson Reuters followed up in 2019 with a survey of thirty-three professionals composed primarily of hiring managers of (1) in-house counsel, (2) outside counsel, and (3) new law school graduates.[8] Table 3 summarizes the responses to the survey.

Table 4 on the succeeding page is the authors' synthesis of the Thomson Reuters interview and survey data.

In October of 2019, the Institute for the Advancement of American Legal Studies (IAALS) published a major study on the competencies that clients want.[9] Partnering with Avvo, IAALS identified a random sample of 2,232 client reviews of lawyers out of 669,255 reviews published by AVVO in the period

---

[6] ROADMAP, *supra* note 2, at 33; *see* Schultz & Zedeck, *supra* note 3, at 630; FOUNDATIONS FOR PRACTICE, *supra* note 5, at 14–16, 20.

[7] Natalie Runyon, *Delta Model Update: The Most Important Area of Lawyer Competency – Personal Effectiveness Skills*, THOMSON REUTERS (Mar. 21, 2019), https://www.legalexecutiveinstitute.com/delta-model-personal-effectiveness-skills/.

[8] NATALIE RUNYON & ALYSON CARREL, ADAPTING FOR TWENTY-FIRST CENTURY SUCCESS: THE DELTA LAWYER COMPETENCY MODEL 2, 8 (2019), https://legal.thomsonreuters.com/content/dam/ewp-m/documents/legal/en/pdf/white-papers/delta-lawyer-competency.pdf.

[9] *See* LOGAN CORNETT, THINK LIKE A CLIENT (2019), https://iaals.du.edu/sites/default/files/documents/publications/think_like_a_client.pdf.

TABLE 2 *Thomson Reuters interviews: What are the top ten competencies that are needed for a successful twenty-first century lawyer?*[10]

Competency	Percentage of Respondents Indicating a Top-Ten Competency
Relationship management	92
Communication (knowing your audience)	83
Project management	83
Emotional intelligence[11]	75
Business fundamentals	67
Entrepreneurial mindset	66
Data analytics	50
Staying current in the law regarding practice areas of expertise	"many" but less than 50%

TABLE 3 *Thomson Reuters surveys: What are the top ten competencies that are needed for a successful twenty-first century lawyer?*[12]

Competency	Percentage of Respondents Rating the Skill as Extremely Important (8–10 on a 10-point scale)
Entrepreneurial mindset and adaptability	91
Legal judgment	67
Legal analysis	63
Pro-active problem solving	61
Legal subject expertise	60
Emotional intelligence (self-management, self-awareness, and empathy)	59
Communication (including active listening)	55
Legal writing	55
Character (honoring commitments)	55
Business fundamentals (and understanding how the client makes money)	48
Relationship management	45
Legal research	42
Project management and technology	42
Data analytics	less than 33

---

[10] Runyon, *supra* note 7.

[11] Emotional intelligence includes self-awareness, self-regulation, and empathy that lead to a lawyer's service as a trusted adviser for a client. *Id.*

[12] DELTA LAWYER COMPETENCY MODEL, *supra* note 8, at 8–10.

TABLE 4 *Synthesis of the Thomson Reuters interview and survey data: Top competencies needed for a successful twenty-first century lawyer*[13]

1. Technical legal skills
  a. Legal judgment
  b. Legal analysis
  c. Legal subject expertise
  d. Legal writing and research
2. Entrepreneurial mindset and adaptability to serve clients and legal employers in changing markets (including project management and technology to lower costs)
3. Client service orientation
  a. Communication (including active listening and knowing your audience)
  b. Relationship management
  c. Knowledge of business fundamentals (including understanding how the client makes money)
  d. Emotional intelligence (including self-management, self-awareness, and empathy)
  e. Character (including honoring commitments)
  f. Proactive problem solving

2007 to 2017.[14] The Advancement of American Legal Studies identified the lawyer competencies that appeared in five percent or more of the reviews in the sample and commented that "each of the[se competencies] appears to have an impact on the client's experience."[15] However, IAALS was not able to indicate the relative importance of each competency.[16] Table 5 on the next page summarizes the IAALS data.

Several other recent empirical studies confirm the Thomson Reuters and IAALS studies' emphasis on client service orientation skills as very important for twenty-first century clients.[17] Table 6 outlines the results of the 2019 BTI Consulting Group's Client Service A-Team Survey of Law Firm Client Service Performance that includes data from 350 in-depth telephone interviews with senior in-house counsel at large organizations.[18]

---

[13] *See* Runyon, *supra* note 7; DELTA LAWYER COMPETENCY MODEL, *supra* note 8.
[14] THINK LIKE A CLIENT, *supra* note 9, at 4.
[15] *See id.* at 3.
[16] *Id.*
[17] *See* Runyon, *supra* note 7; DELTA LAWYER COMPETENCY MODEL, *supra* note 8, at 8–10; THINK LIKE A CLIENT, *supra* note 9, at 3–4; BTI CONSULTING GROUP, BTI CLIENT SERVICE A-TEAM 2019: SURVEY OF LAW FIRM CLIENT SERVICE PERFORMANCE (2019), https://bticonsulting.com/themadclientist/bti-client-service-a-team-2019-survey-of-law-firm-client-service-performance [hereinafter BTI SURVEY].
[18] BTI SURVEY, *supra* note 17. The BTI Consulting's 18th Annual Client Service All-Stars 2019, based on the same telephone interview data, reports that the all-stars identified by clients provide

TABLE 5 *IAALS's analysis to identify the lawyer competencies that appeared in 5 percent or more of the AVVO reviews of lawyers in the period 2007–2017*[19]

1. **Communications with the client, including:**
   a. Promptness of response
   b. Provision of status updates
   c. Explanation of the matter and potential courses of action
   d. Degree of accessibility
2. **Interpersonal behavior with the client, including:**
   a. Qualities associated with trustworthiness, integrity, and reliability
   b. Professionalism (undefined)
   c. Ability to relate to the client with tolerance, sensitivity, and compassion
   d. Sociability
   e. Taking a personal interest in the matter
   f. Respect and courtesy to the client
3. **Value of the lawyer's contribution to the client's matter, including specific outcomes and the cost of the services**
4. **Technical lawyering skills**
5. **Tenacity, including diligence and work ethic**

Note that the respondents in this survey indicated that legal skills and quality work are important to get in the door for consideration but they are not differentiating. Both are expected and abundant in the market.[20]

    (1) "superior client focus" (including achieving the best outcome from the client's unique perspective);

    (2) "unmatched client experience" (including identifying business risks and helping inside counsel shape messages for management);

    (3) "understanding the client's business like no other" (including discussing "how legal advice will impact business goals" and proactive monitoring and advice on business and industry risks);

    (4) "unparalleled legal skills" (including "identify[ing] and discuss[ing] legal needs before a major issue arises"); and

    (5) "innovative thought leadership" (including "educat[ing] the client on how to manage risks associated with emerging issues").

Based on the results of its 2018 survey, BTI's most important recommendation to deliver superior service is to "ingrain yourself in the [client's] business – not [just] the [immediate] matter .... Cloak all your recommendations and guidance in the context of the client's business. Legal decision makers say business context most differentiates one attorney from another .... The work is important, but is only one component of a successful relationship. Many attorneys are capable of providing effective counsel. Few focus on building the business relationship .... Teach clients something they don't know that will help them do their job better .... No charge. Taking a step to prove you are invested in the client earns you their investment back." BTI CONSULTING GROUP, BTI CLIENT SERVICE ALL-STARS FOR LAW FIRMS 57 (2018).

[19] *See* THINK LIKE A CLIENT, *supra* note 9, at 6–17.
[20] *See* BTI SURVEY, *supra* note 17, at 8.

TABLE 6 *2019 BTI Consulting Group survey of law firm client service performance*
(350 interviews with senior in-house counsel)[21]
The top differentiating skills driving superior client relationships are

(1) Commitment to help (matching the client's emotional investment in a matter);
(2) client focus (being responsive to a client's needs and goals);
(3) understanding the client's business (better understanding leads to more relevant advice); and
(4) providing value for the dollar (delivering more than the client expects).

Therefore, fostering these differentiating skills and superior relationship skills should be a major point of emphasis to prepare law students for successful acquisition and retention of legal jobs after graduation.

Similarly, the Altman Weil 2018 Chief Legal Officer Survey of 279 law department leaders found the most important efforts outside counsel could make to improve relations with the client were all related to improved responsiveness to the client's needs, including "[g]reater cost reduction," "[n]on-hourly based pricing structures," improved budget forecasting so the client will know what the service will cost, "[m]ore efficient project management," modification of work to match the legal risk involved, "[i]mproved communication and responsiveness," and greater effort to understand the client's business.[22] Furthermore, the 2019 Association of Corporate Counsel survey of 1,639 respondents who identified themselves as the highest-ranking lawyer in a company[23] reported that the top non-legal skills that chief legal officers want for the in-house legal team are: (1) leadership; (2) business management skills; (3) communication and listening skills; (4) project management skills; and (5) presentation skills.[24]

In 2020, the National Conference of Bar Examiners published a survey of 3,153 newly licensed lawyers (up to 3 years of practice) and 11,693 non-recently licensed lawyers asking how frequently newly licensed lawyers performed specifically listed tasks.[25] The study included the combined ranking of both

[21]   *Id.*
[22]   *See* ALTMAN WEIL INC., 2018 CHIEF LEGAL OFFICER SURVEY viii, 45 (2018), http://www.altmanweil.com//dir_docs/resource/D3942AD5-753D-4EDC-96C6-99048671F193_document.pdf.
[23]   ASS'N CORP. COUNS., 2019 ACC CHIEF LEGAL OFFICERS SURVEY 2 (2019), https://www.acc.com/sites/default/files/resources/upload/2019-ACC-Chief-Legal-Officers-Survey.pdf.
[24]   *See id.* at 21–22.
[25]   NAT'L CONF. BAR EXAMINERS TESTING TASK FORCE, PHASE 2 REPORT: 2019 PRACTICE ANALYSIS (2020).

TABLE 7 *2020 NCBE Survey Ranking of the Most Critical Skills and Abilities for Newly Licensed Lawyers*

1. Written/reading comprehension
2. Analytical thinking
3. Written expression
4. Identifying legal issues
5. Integrity/honesty
6. Conscientiousness
7. Professionalism – demonstrate respect for the profession with civility and candor
8. Adapting to change, pressure, and setbacks
9. Fact gathering
10. Oral comprehension
11. Advocacy – written and oral
12. Attentive to details
13. Practical judgment
14. Diligence and persistence
15. Collegiality to establish quality relationships and work collaboratively
16. Legal research
17. Oral expression
18. Continuous learning
19. Managing projects
20. Collaboration/Teamwork to accomplish a common goal

groups with respect to the criticality (low, medium, or high) of a list of skills and abilities for newly licensed lawyers.[26] Table 7 indicates the ranking of the top twenty most critical skills and abilities.

In 2020, the California State Bar published the results of a survey of 16,190 California attorneys to collect data on (1) what attorneys do as reflected in daily tasks, and (2) what knowledge attorneys use to perform those tasks.[27] The survey was administered to gauge the alignment between the content of the California Bar Exam and the practice of law in California. In addition to making recommendations on the legal topics to be included on the bar exam, the report recommended a list of competencies to be considered for inclusion on the bar exam as follows:[28]

– Drafting and writing;
– Research and investigation;

[26]   *Id.* at 62.
[27]   STATE BAR OF CALIFORNIA CAPA WORKING GROUP, THE PRACTICE OF LAW IN CALIFORNIA: FINDINGS FROM THE CALIFORNIA ATTORNEY PRACTICE ANALYSIS AND IMPLICATIONS FOR THE CALIFORNIA BAR EXAM (2020).
[28]   *Id.* at 18–19.

- Issue-spotting and fact-gathering;
- Counsel/advice;
- Litigation;
- Communication and client relationship including:
  ~ Establishing the client relationship;
  ~ Maintaining the client relationship; and
  ~ Communication.

In 2020, IAALS published another national study based on 50 focus groups that were asked about the knowledge and skills that new lawyers used during the first year of practice.[29] From the focus group data, Merritt and Cornett identified 12 building blocks that allowed the new lawyers possessing these abilities to represent clients with little or no supervision. The 12 building blocks are set forth in Table 8. The order of the building blocks does not indicate their relative importance. The authors thought all of them are critical components of minimum competence for a new lawyer.[30]

TABLE 8 IAALS 2020 *Twelve Building Blocks of Minimum Competence for a New Lawyer*

1. The ability to act professionally and in accordance with the Rules of Professional Conduct
2. An understanding of legal process and the sources of law
3. An understanding of the threshold concepts in many subjects
4. The ability to interpret legal materials
5. The ability to interact effectively with clients
6. The ability to identify legal issues
7. The ability to conduct research
8. The ability to communicate as a lawyer
9. The ability to understand the big picture of client matters
10. The ability to manage a law-related workload responsibly
11. The ability to cope with the stress of legal practice
12. The ability to pursue self-directed learning.

[29] DEBORAH JONES MERRITT & LOGAN CORNETT, BUILDING A BETTER BAR: THE TWELVE BUILDING BLOCKS OF MINIMUM COMPETENCE 14–15 (2020) (the study had 200 total participants with 41 focus groups of junior lawyers who had been licensed between Jan. 1, 2016, and Jan. 31, 2019, and had worked at least 12 months in one or more positions that required a law license, and 9 focus groups of experienced lawyers who had supervised at least one junior lawyer during the two years preceding the study).

[30] *Id.* at 31.

In 2021, Mitt Regan and Lisa Rohrer published a study (summarized in Table 9) reporting on in-depth interviews with 278 law partners at larger US law firms to assess whether business concerns are eclipsing professional values in law firm practice.[31]

In 2020–21, IAALS conducted collaborative working sessions with 36 different legal employers in New York, Chicago, Denver, and Seattle representing a variety of practice areas and organization sizes. IAALS then synthesized the working session results with the data from its 2016 Foundations for Practice survey of more than 24,000 lawyers from across the country. In its publication *Foundations Instructional Design Guide*, IAALS draws on that research to recommend five Foundations Learning Outcomes to help schools instill and measure what is important for student practice-readiness, and help

TABLE 9 *Competencies Highlighted in Regan and Rohrer's Interviews with 278 Law Firm Partners*

1. Although at an earlier time, big firm lawyers were acculturated that excellence in the craft of lawyering defined by internal professional standards would provide assurance of advancement and financial success, the firms now are emphasizing that lawyers need to be more entrepreneurial because of increasing competitive pressure.[32]
2. Professional values contributing to each lawyer's meaning in the work are still important to many partners.[33]
3. Many partners indicated that serving as a trusted advisor for their clients is how they can play a distinctive role as a professional.[34] Commitment to the client (being client-centered) is essential in this role, but the lawyers also counsel beyond technical legality to include the spirit of the law and broader considerations, sometime expressed in the client's risk language, from a deep understanding of the client's context and business.[35]
4. Building and sustaining a cooperative firm culture can create a competitive advantage for a firm. Being both entrepreneurial and collaborative within the firm is very important.[36]

---

[31] MITT REGAN & LISA ROHRER, BIG LAW: MONEY AND MEANING IN THE MODERN LAW FIRM 2 (2021).

[32] *Id.* at 2, 5. Regan and Rohrer find that responses from partners across all firms emphasize the common critical challenge posed by intensifying competition and pressure for financial performance. *Id.*

[33] *Id.* at 244–45, 233. The interviews indicated that law firm partners in bigger firms seek both money and meaning in their practice. They still maintain a sense of themselves as a distinctive profession notwithstanding a significant intensification of business pressures in recent years. *Id.*

[34] *Id.* at 231.

[35] *Id.* at 228, 230–31, 204–05, 212–17.

[36] *Id.* 7–8, 239.

employers adopt hiring practices that identify candidates that they want to hire and retain.[37]

> COMMUNICATOR – Communicate by reading, writing, speaking, and listening in a professional manner.
>
> PRACTITIONER – Employ research, synthesize, analyze, and apply skills in legal processes and actions.
>
> PROFESSIONAL – Use efficient methods and tools to manage one's and the firm or organization's professional workload with accuracy and utility.
>
> PROBLEM SOLVER – Solve long-term and immediate problems to the benefit of all stakeholders.
>
> SELF STARTER – Demonstrate leadership, responsibility, and initiative in work responsibilities with little supervision.

In 2021, the National Association for Law Placement published a survey of 58 large firms where 51 (88 percent) indicated they do have competency models for associate assessment.[38] Fifty of the firms provided data on the competencies included in their models. Competencies included in more than 80 percent of the firm models are listed as follows here.

Competency	No. of firms including this competency
Legal analysis	49
Written advocacy	49
Communicating clearly	49
Legal knowledge	48
Judgment/common sense	48
Teamwork/collaboration	48
Oral advocacy	47
Initiative	47
Responsibility/reliability	47
Responsiveness to client	47
Understand client's business/circumstances	47
Attention to detail	47
Leadership	44

---

[37] IAALS, FOUNDATIONS INSTRUCTIONAL DESIGN GUIDE 14 (2021), https://iaals.du.edu/sites/default/files/documents/publications/foundations_instructional_design_guide.pdf.

[38] NAT'L ASS'N L. PLACEMENT, REPORT ON 2020 SURVEY OF LAW FIRM COMPETENCY EXPECTATIONS FOR ASSOCIATE DEVELOPMENT 5–6 (2021), https://www.nalp.org/uploads/NALP_Associate_Competencies_Report_May_2021.pdf.

(*continued*)

Competency	No. of firms including this competency
Legal research	43
Problem-solving	42
Respect for others	40

The major futurists looking at the legal services market emphasize that the competencies needed for a successful twenty-first century lawyer include a more pro-active entrepreneurial mindset to meet changing market conditions for the clients and the lawyers.[39] Richard Susskind highlights the "more for less" challenge, in which clients want legal services delivered at lower cost, and the related challenge of taking advantage of the increasing capabilities of information technology to streamline current processes in legal services.[40] Jordan Furlong and William Henderson also emphasize that client demands for better, faster, and cheaper legal services are causing a structural change in the legal services market.[41] To thrive in the years ahead, lawyers will need to become more entrepreneurial, more efficient, and less expensive through the use of new technologies and collaboration.[42] They stress the need for both project management skills and collaboration skills in teams of lawyers, nonlawyers, and clients to achieve greater efficiencies and lower costs.[43]

Client surveys accentuate the importance of client orientation and relationship skills. Randall Kiser, in his 2017 book *Soft Skills for the Effective Lawyer*, notes that while both attorneys and clients include client service orientation and relationship skills among the important competencies needed to represent clients, the clients emphasize these skills (including communication, attentive listening, responsiveness, understanding of client's context and business, and explanation of fee arrangements) more heavily.[44]

---

[39] *See* RICHARD SUSSKIND, TOMORROW'S LAWYERS: AN INTRODUCTION TO YOUR FUTURE 4–14 (2013); William Henderson, *Efficiency Engines: How Managed Services Are Building Systems for Corporate Legal Work*, ABA J. 38–45 (June 2017); JORDAN FURLONG, LAW IS A BUYER'S MARKET: BUILDING A CLIENT-FIRST LAW FIRM 29, 73–81, 145–52 (2017).

[40] TOMORROW'S LAWYERS, *supra* note 39, at 4–14.

[41] Henderson, *supra* note 39, at 38–45; LAW IS A BUYER'S MARKET *supra* note 39, at 29, 73–81, 145–52.

[42] *See supra* note 41, and sources cited therein.

[43] *See supra* note 41, and sources cited therein.

[44] RANDALL KISER, SOFT SKILLS FOR THE EFFECTIVE LAWYER 32–33 (2017).

2

A Framework for Purposefulness to Realize the Four
Professional Development and Formation Goals

In 2007, the Carnegie Foundation for the Advancement of Teaching published its influential study of legal education, *Educating Lawyers*.[1] In stressing that the formation of professional identity and purpose is central to the development of law students into lawyers,[2] *Educating Lawyers* introduced new language to the legal academy – but not a new mission. For generations, law schools have proclaimed the goal of graduating well-rounded and well-grounded new lawyers who have made good progress toward their socialization in the legal profession.[3] The problem that *Educating Lawyers* perceived was the failure of law schools to pursue the professional formation dimension of their educational work with anything like the intentionality and drive for excellence they exhibit

---

Many of the ideas and materials presented in this chapter are drawn from Louis D. Bilionis, *Bringing Purposefulness to the American Law School's Support of Professional Identity Formation*, 14 U. St. Thomas L. J. 480 (2018), and Louis D. Bilionis, *Law School Leadership and Leadership Development for Developing Lawyers*, 58 Santa Clara L. Rev. 601 (2018).

[1] William M. Sullivan et al., Educating Lawyers: Preparation for the Profession of Law (2007) [hereinafter Educating Lawyers].

[2] *Id.* at 28, 129.

[3] We are speaking of law schools in their institutional capacity. Some law professors are uncertain of the role they personally can play in their students' development of a professional identity and sense of purpose. Faculty also may wonder whether professional identity formation implicates contestable values that should be left to the student personally, as well as whether they as faculty members possess expertise in the matter. *See, e.g.,* Roger C. Cramton, *The Ordinary Religion of the Law School Classroom*, 29 J. Legal Educ. 247, 253 (1978); Educating Lawyers, *supra* note 1, at 132–33 (noting "the strong impression that in most law schools, the apprenticeship of professionalism and purpose is subordinated to the cognitive, academic apprenticeship" and that "in the minds of many faculty, ethical and social values are subjective and indeterminate and, for that reason, can potentially even conflict with the all-important values of the academy – values that underlie the cognitive apprenticeship: rigor, skepticism, intellectual distance, and objectivity").

when helping students to think like a lawyer.[4] Professional formation was left much to chance. It was the hoped-for consequence of the student's travails in the bramble bush that is American legal education.[5]

An all-important ingredient – *purposefulness* – has been missing. This book details how law schools can provide it, and we begin in this chapter with a framework to help faculty and staff bring that purposefulness to their support of professional formation. We introduce some ways to think about law students, their law school, and American legal education that we hope faculty and staff will find invigorating. There is no call to abandon prevailing approaches to the cognitive and skills dimensions of a law student's education that *Educating Lawyers* labeled the first and second apprenticeships, respectively.[6] But when it comes to professional identity formation, the third apprenticeship, a shift in perspective will reveal opportunities with time,

---

[4] *See* EDUCATING LAWYERS, *supra* note 1, at 128 (concluding that "law schools need to further deepen their knowledge of how the apprenticeship of professionalism and purpose works ... improve their understanding of their own formative capacity, including learning from their own strengths, as well as those of other professions ... [and] attend more systematically to the pedagogical practices that foster the formation of integrated, responsible lawyers").

[5] *Cf.* K. N. Llewellyn, The Bramble Bush 112 (2008) (1930) (describing the law as "the thicket of thorns" and the study of the law as "[h]igh sun, no path, no light, thirst and the thorns"). Karl Llewellyn's classic advice to students was total immersion in the traditional law school's rigorous cognitive curriculum and cocurricular experiences like law review that emphasize cognitive skills:

> Eat law, talk law, think law, drink law, babble of law and judgments in your sleep. Pickle yourselves in law – it is your only hope. And to do this you need more than your classes and your casebooks, and yourselves. You need your fellows. You need your neighbor on the right .... All of this becomes fairly obvious if you but glance at some of the things which go to make up the practice of the law.

Id. at 102; *see also* Thomas L. Shaffer & Robert S. Redmount, *Legal Education: The Classroom Experience*, 52 NOTRE DAME LAW 190 (1976):

> American legal education has always said or implied that its commodity is the graduate who can be a good lawyer, and that nothing but American legal education itself is capable of producing this commodity .... The point here is neither the claim nor the fact that the criterion is self-referring; the task is to describe the system as it is described to beginning law students. That description is that their professionalism will come as a result of enduring the law-school process, but not as a result of any discrete part of the process. It will not come, for instance, as a result of assimilating information. Nor will it come as a result of taking courses (even though the visible substance of legal education is almost all in courses). Nor will it come as a result of the direct effect of modelling one's behavior on professors .... What appears to be the heart of this communication is that if one works very hard the commodity will appear.

Id. at 192.

[6] *See* EDUCATING LAWYERS, *supra* note 1, at 28 (describing the intellectual and cognitive first apprenticeship of the law student's development and the "second apprenticeship ... of expert practice shared by competent practitioners").

talent, space, and experiences. It can leave faculty and staff with a justified sense of optimism that effective support of professional identity formation is within reach.

2.1 HOW TO THINK ABOUT PROFESSIONAL IDENTITY FORMATION

2.1.1 *Choose a Workable Conception of Professional Identity*

Purposefulness means being intentional about the right things, about focusing on the appropriate goals. Purposefulness about the formation of professional identity starts with a clear idea about what *professional identity* entails.

Educators in medical schools employ a definition that translates well to law: professional identity is "a representation of self, achieved in stages over time, during which the characteristics, values, and norms of the medical [or legal] profession are internalized, resulting in an individual thinking, acting, and feeling like a physician [or lawyer]."[7] For legal education, we recommended in Chapter 1 viewing professional identity as the student's accepted and internalized

- Ownership of continuous professional development toward excellence at the major competencies that clients, employers, and the legal system need;
- a deep responsibility and service orientation to others, especially the client;
- a client-centered, problem-solving approach and good judgment that ground the student's responsibility and service to the client; and
- well-being practices.

This formulation of a lawyer's professional identity rests on propositions rooted in the legal profession's social contract and in a lawyer's own self-interest in professional success: the expectation of excellence in the service provided to others and the necessity of the lawyer's ongoing capacity to provide it. It is a general definition that references without specification "major competencies" that will require elaboration, and we will touch on what that means for the work of a law school in Section 2.1.3 and explore the issue extensively in Chapters 3 and 4. But at the outset, note how this conception of professional identity avoids distracting debates over subjective values[8] while inviting

---

[7]   Richard L. Cruess et al., *Reframing Medical Education to Support Professional Identity Formation*, 89 ACAD. MED. 1446, 1447 (2014).

[8]   For an exploration of alternative conceptions and definitions of professionalism, see Neil Hamilton, *Professionalism Clearly Defined*, 18 PROF. LAW 4 (2008) (surveying academic

recognition of attributes like self-direction, leadership-of-self, and commitment to improvement that are as indispensable to a lawyer's professional identity as they are critical to a law student's success in school and in the employment marketplace. It is a unifying and workable definition in the law school setting.

As we noted in Chapter 1, this formulation also is a statement of four goals – the PD&F goals – for students to pursue. If any of the four PD&F goals has support among faculty, staff, or administrators at a particular law school, that school is poised to move forward in a purposeful fashion. As we discuss in Chapter 5, a key initial step is to assess the school's local conditions to gauge faculty, staff, and administrator interest in these goals. With interest identified, a "coalition of the willing" can be formed to pursue a number of recommended steps to purposefully strengthen the school's support of student progress toward the goals.

2.1.2 *See the Formation of Professional Identity as Principally a Process of Socialization*

A purposeful effort to support the formation of professional identity needs not only a workable conception of professional identity but also a solid sense of what *formation* means. Medical educators envision identity formation as principally a process of socialization[9] – an understanding that should resonate with lawyers and law professors. The professional-to-be begins as an outsider to the professional community and its ways, values, and norms. Through experiences over time, the individual gradually becomes more and more an insider, "moving from a stance of observer on the outside or periphery of the practice through graduated stages toward becoming a skilled participant at the center of the action."[10] The process continues throughout one's career[11] and features "a series of identity transformations that occur primarily during periods of

and professional organization discussions of core values of the profession and offering a synthesis).

[9]   *See, e.g.,* Cruess et al., *supra* note 7, at 1448.

[10]   William M. Sullivan, *Foreword to* TEACHING MEDICAL PROFESSIONALISM: SUPPORTING THE DEVELOPMENT OF A PROFESSIONAL IDENTITY ix, xii (Richard L. Cruess et al. eds., 2d ed. 2016) [hereinafter TEACHING MEDICAL PROFESSIONALISM]; *see also* Frederic William Hafferty, *Socialization, Professionalism, and Professional Identity Formation, in* TEACHING MEDICAL PROFESSIONALISM, at 55, 62.

[11]   Lynn V. Monrouxe, *Theoretical Insights into the Nature and Nurture of Professional Identities, in* TEACHING MEDICAL PROFESSIONALISM, *supra* note 10, at 37, 38 ("Our identities are continually *rewritten* throughout our lives as we draw on the environment, from people and from objects for their content.")

transition"[12] marked by anxiety, stress, and risk for the developing professional.[13] Educational theorists call the learning that occurs in this process of socialization "contextually situated"[14] – the product of the developing lawyer's social interactions and activities in environments authentic to the legal profession's culture and enriched by coaching, mentoring, modeling, reflection, and other supportive strategies.[15]

The periods of transition that students experience stand out as important focal points for purposeful formation support – a principle we will explore more extensively in Chapter 4.[16] Law schools can identify the important transitions their students experience and tailor strategies to better support students through them. A good picture of the transition periods and their effect on competencies also can reveal developmental experiences that are missing and should be provided.[17]

2.1.3 *Recognize the Components of Professional Identity Formation and the Interrelationship between Them – and the Significance of Competencies*

Newcomers to purposeful work in support of the professional identity formation of law students will encounter new topics and terms, and even different language to refer to the same concept. Legal educators come to the formation project from different starting points and with different understandings, expectations, and aspirations. There are many on-ramps to the work of supporting the student's formation of professional identity.

There are staples of purposeful formation work, however, and it pays to locate them conceptually and appreciate the interrelationship between them. Here is a way of mapping them within the professional identity framework. The definition of professional identity that we recommend begins with a first foundational goal that calls on each student to develop toward excellence at all the major competencies of the profession. What are the major competencies of the profession to which this first PD&F goal alludes? How do those

---

[12]   Robert Sternszus, *Developing a Professional Identity: A Learner's Perspective*, in Teaching Medical Professionalism, *supra* note 10, at 26, 31.

[13]   *See* Cruess et al., *supra* note 7, at 1448; *see also* Monrouxe, *supra* note 11, at 43.

[14]   *See* Yvonne Steinert, *Educational Theory and Strategies to Support Professionalism and Identity Formation*, in Teaching Medical Professionalism, *supra* note 10, at 68, 69–71.

[15]   *See, e.g., id.; see also* Cruess et al., *supra* note 7, at 1448.

[16]   *See* Sternszus, *supra* note 12, at 29–30, 33. See *infra* Chapter 4 discussion at principle 6, for more discussion of the importance of transitions in the formation of a student's professional identity.

[17]   The goal is to "take explicit steps to coordinate the multiplicity of learning environments ... [in order to] produce a professionally infused tapestry." Hafferty, *supra* note 10, at 59.

competencies relate to the other three foundational PD&F goals? And how do the PD&F goals relate to one another?

Figure 2 depicts the interrelationships among the four goals and all the other major competencies needed to be successful in the practice of law. Developed by a working group of the Holloran Center for Ethical Leadership in the Professions at the University of St. Thomas School of Law in Minneapolis, Minnesota, the model in Figure 2 includes all the competencies clients and legal employers need that were summarized in Chapter 1 and its Appendix, reorganized here into a progression of building blocks.

Figure 2's Group 1 competencies make clear that new entrants into the legal profession (and, indeed, into all the professions) must internalize the first two foundational PD&F goals. Ownership of continuous professional development toward excellence at the major competencies and a deep responsibility and service orientation to others are essential to the developing professional's progress toward achieving all the remaining particularized competencies in Groups 2 through 5. They are the heart of "being" a lawyer.

The Group 2 competencies include cognitive skills that legal education traditionally has prioritized and practical skills that law schools have emphasized increasingly in recent decades. These correspond to the first and second apprenticeships identified in *Educating Lawyers*[18] and might be rendered colloquially as the skills that go into "thinking" and "doing" like a lawyer. Group 3 introduces to the picture a number of basic individual and relational building-block competencies, starting with the foundational PD&F competency (and goal) of well-being practices. Group 4 recognizes "compound competencies" that apply and build upon the foregoing. One such compound competency is client-centered problem solving – our third foundational PD&F competency (and goal). Group 5 acknowledges that there are yet more, and more complex, compound competencies that involve application of the foregoing competencies in settings and contexts that raise special challenges. The reader can see in Groups 1 through 5 that one or another of these diverse competencies might be of special interest to particular faculty, staff, or administrators at one's own law school. As we have said, there are many on-ramps into the work of fostering the formation of each student's professional identity.

No generally agreed-upon catalogue of all the competencies that one might locate in Figure 2 exists, and the law school has choices to make in creating the list of competencies that it will make the focus of its work in helping its students. Some competencies might be included because clients and legal

---

[18] See *supra* note 6 and accompanying text.

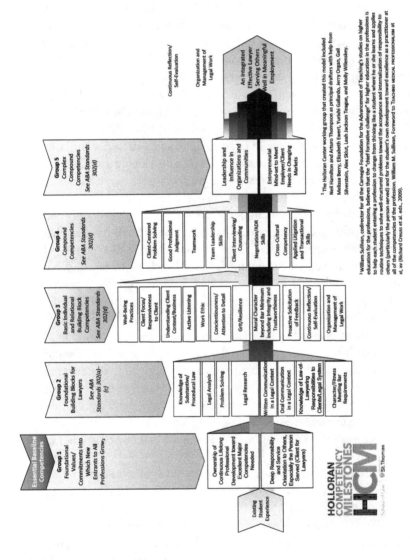

FIGURE 2 How the competencies that legal employers and client want build on each other

employers affirm them as important to a lawyer's success in the practice of law (as demonstrated, for instance, by the data reflected in Figure 1 in Chapter 1). Other competencies may be included because they appear in law school accreditation standards, requirements for admission to the bar, or applicable codes of ethics and professionalism.[19] Competencies also might merit inclusion because the faculty and staff believe the legal profession's social contract calls for them, even if neither regulation nor the marketplace has so spoken. From the standpoint of ensuring purposefulness, the actual choices that the law school makes here matter less than the reasons for them. Let those reasons be clear and honest and open and accountable to the interests of all concerned, including students and external stakeholders who entrust law schools with the responsibility for legal education.

When the law school is identifying competencies, there likely will be references made to so-called hard skills and soft skills. Shorthand has its place, but a caution about its use here is in order. Labeling competencies as "hard" or "soft" involves neither science nor art, and the use of such labels can lead to unconscious indirection and the introduction of unspoken new considerations. Do the adjectives "hard" and "soft" suggest something about the comparative worth of the skill? If so, by what measures and according to whose values? Do the adjectives mean something about comparative rigor? If so, rigor on what axis, and with what relevancy to someone's development as a lawyer? Do they refer to comparative amenability to teaching? If so, by what calculation, upon what assumptions about what it means to teach, and again with what relevancy? Using and giving weight to the labels "hard" and "soft," without uncovering the premises and connotations that the adjectives might be masking, only makes purposefulness harder to attain. Better to steer clear of the adjectives and get to the real points instead.

Among competencies, the capacity for self-direction (sometimes addressed as self-directed learning, self-regulated learning, self-awareness, or leadership-of-self) occupies a crucial place because so much else turns on it.[20]

---

[19] See, e.g., *2021–2022 Standards and Rules of Procedure for Approval of Law Schools*, A.B.A. SECTION OF LEGAL EDUC. & ADMISSIONS TO THE BAR (Standard 302 (requiring and specifying learning outcomes); Standard 314 (requiring assessment of student learning); Standard 315 (requiring evaluation of program of legal education, learning outcomes, and assessment methods)); Hamilton, *supra* note 8 (reviewing requirements set forth in professional codes and bar admissions).

[20] Chapter 1's discussion of the benefits of PD&F goal 1 lists the benefits of student growth to later stages of self-directed learning. *See also* MALCOLM KNOWLES, SELF-DIRECTED LEARNING: A GUIDE FOR LEARNERS AND TEACHERS 18 (1975) (defining self-directed learning as "a process in which individuals take the initiative, with or without the help of others, in diagnosing their learning needs, formulating learning goals, identifying the human and

The professional's ability to pursue and maintain excellence depends on it, as does one's ability to serve others responsibly and to provide leadership. Before serving and leading others, one must first be able to serve and lead oneself.[21] Research indicates that many law students are at relatively early stages of development with respect to self-direction[22] – making it all the more deserving of the law school's attention. Faculty may not use the term self-direction, but they have the concept in mind when they contrast the unfocused, struggling student with the successful one who has command of law school's challenges. Advisors in academic success programs have the concept in mind daily in their work, as do career services counselors when they report that students who take insufficient personal ownership of their job searches face greater difficulty obtaining meaningful employment upon graduation. A law school that prioritizes student success will not overlook self-direction and associated capacities like resourcefulness, resilience, and critical reflexivity.[23] The school also will recognize that faculty and staff across the enterprise can contribute to and profit from the school's efforts to support development of these competencies.

An important final point about competencies: to say that a law school can improve its support of student professional identity formation by focusing more explicitly and purposefully on competencies is not the same thing as saying the school must adopt "competency-based learning" as its educational model. Under the competency-based learning model, a student progresses through a course of study by demonstrating proficiency at increasing staged levels of designated competencies – and not, as progress is structured under the traditional educational model of law schools, by accumulating credit

---

material resources for learning, choosing and implementing appropriate learning strategies, and evaluating learning outcomes").

[21]   See Sullivan, *supra* note 10, at xiv (noting that "a strong professional identity requires that students develop a proactive stance toward their own learning and career choices" and that being a "self-directed learner ... [is] an essential quality for a successful later life" as a professional).

[22]   See Neil Hamilton, *A Professional Formation/Professionalism Challenge: Many Students Need Help with Self-Directed Learning Concerning Their Professional Development Toward Excellence*, 27 REGENT U. L. REV. 225, 230–36 (2014).

[23]   See, e.g., Brian D. Hodges, *Professional Identities of the Future: Invisible and Unconscious or Deliberate and Reflexive, in* TEACHING MEDICAL PROFESSIONALISM, *supra* note 10, at 277, 283–85 (advocating a professional's need for "critical reflexivity" to meet future challenges; "[i]f we are to realize a future in which the formation of identities is deliberate and reflexive, watchwords for educators in the twenty-first century will need to be *adaptive expertise, metacognition, cognitive flexibility,* and *critical reflexivity*"); Cruess et al., *supra* note 7, at 1450 (noting that "although there are clearly core elements that are foundational and seem to be timeless, some aspects of the traditional professional identity must change").

hours that reflect time spent on various subjects.[24] As Chapter 3 explains, medical education has adopted the competency-based model and trends in American education suggest it is taking hold widely. The American Bar Association recently introduced accreditation standards that move law schools in that direction but, in application, stop short of full adoption of the model. For our purposes, it suffices to note that every school can profit by bringing purposefulness to its support of professional identity formation. Successful initiatives can be launched within either model and adapted easily for use in the other.

2.2 HOW TO THINK – AND NOT THINK – ABOUT SUPPORTING PROFESSIONAL IDENTITY FORMATION

It is human to make assumptions that frame issues in ways that misdirect us or obscure possibilities. Four framing assumptions, reflecting familiar under-standings about legal education, can distort a law school's thinking about how to support professional formation. Examining them will bring to the fore new ways of thinking that better serve purposeful and effective efforts.

2.2.1 *Think First and Foremost of the Student's Socialization and Formation Experiences: What Law Faculty Do Is Important, but Only One of Many Means to the End*

When law professors are asked how their school might be more purposeful in supporting professional formation, their thoughts likely turn immediately to things professors do (and might do differently) in their roles as teachers. There are right times and places for engaging in this reasonable way of thinking, but not at the outset.

This is a more important point than its simplicity might suggest. What law professors do is only a means to the relevant end here – the student's personal development of a professional identity. Analysis that begins with means rather than ends runs the risk of missing the mark. Framing from the faculty perspective, rather than from the student's socialization journey and what it entails, can exclude a world of possibilities from the picture.

Many factors that influence a student's formation of professional identity lie beyond what the law school customarily contemplates legal education to

---

[24] *See, e.g.,* Neil Hamilton, *Leadership of Self: Each Student Taking Ownership Over Continuous Professional Development/Self-Directed Learning,* 58 SANTA CLARA L. REV. 567, 569–72 (2018) (discussing competency-based education, with focus on medical and legal education).

encompass. When it comes to a student's education in legal doctrine and the cognitive competencies of lawyering, the faculty's role is dominant, with staff within the school and individuals and organizations outside the school playing smaller parts, if any. The formation of professional identity, on the other hand, is a socialization process affected by numerous other experiences that have much less to do directly with the professors. Consider student experiences in seeking and obtaining summer and postgraduation employment, or during internships or part-time employment, or in extracurricular activities. Those influential experiences happen at a *time* during the student's law school years preceding professional employment, but not a time that the faculty customarily considers its immediate responsibility. They occur in a *space* that the student frequents during the law school years preceding professional employment, but not a space over which the faculty customarily assumes active jurisdiction. They occur in the proximity of *people* who influence the experience, but they are people other than the student's professors – among them, career counselors, interviewing employers, moot court judges, lawyers in a student's summer workplace or externship placement, attorneys invited to participate in brown bag lunches, formal and informal mentors, and peers on their own professional socialization journey.

Starting from the law faculty perspective constricts legal education's palette, obscuring experiences, time, space, and talent that legal education has within its reach to better support the student's formation of professional identity. It also brings vying priorities and interests to the fore before the potential benefits to student professional identity formation have been fully explored.

2.2.2 *Think about Taking Responsibility and Asserting Leadership: What Law Schools Can Do Is Not Limited to "Teaching" by the Faculty*

Law professors contemplating what their school can do to better help students in their formation of professional identity likely will presuppose that the answers involve some form of transmission of knowledge by the faculty to students. After all, isn't that what teaching is, and isn't teaching what a law school does?

Framing the law school's capacities that way defines legal education and the law school's appropriate functions too narrowly. Teaching as it is customarily envisioned – the transmission of expert knowledge by a professor who imparts doctrinal wisdom and hones student skills in analysis and synthesis – figures enormously. But the education of the American lawyer involves more. Other kinds of experiences are formative for the developing lawyer and thus, in a real and meaningful sense, an integral part of the legal education. The challenge for law schools is twofold: to see legal education in those broader terms and to recognize that society expects law schools to take responsibility for legal education in those broader terms. The social contract will hold law schools responsible for the pre-professional-employment period of a lawyer's development in all its facets.

How do we know? Because law schools already are being held accountable for the outcomes of that developmental period, whether they realize it or not. Today, those outcomes are measured by successful admission to the bar and success in obtaining employment – and the accreditation regime, the rankings and reputational environment, and the admissions marketplace all impose accountability for them. Trends in higher education suggest the future will judge schools by an expanding array of alumni success measures. It is no answer to competitively disadvantageous outcomes that the law school conveys expert knowledge well. Law schools increasingly will be pressed to leave no professional development stone unturned.

Accepting this responsibility means embracing a leadership challenge. The question is not so much what additional expert knowledge the law faculty can convey, but rather what the school as a whole can do to maximize the formative potential of the pre-professional-employment period – what diverse talents, techniques, and resources it can muster and deploy. A purposeful effort will depend on three key steps.

First, it is necessary to be frank about the period for which the law school bears responsibility. The traditional "conveying of expert knowledge" way of thinking marks the start of this period at law school matriculation and its end at graduation, with the summers after the first and second years of law school characterized as "breaks." Law schools now acknowledge, at least implicitly, that the period of their responsibility extends further because they explicitly treat their field of competition and marketplace accountability as extending further. The period really begins not with matriculation but with increasingly intensive recruitment and admissions processes that initiate the student's professional socialization. The period ends not at graduation but with the passing of the bar examination and the securing of a job – activities that law schools support with expanded postgraduation services. And those summers are not "breaks" that punctuate the period but months designated for real-world experiences that schools promote and facilitate, and even create and subsidize, because they are central to development.

The second step is to draw into view the diverse formative experiences that occur (or could occur) in that pre-professional-employment period, together with the varied times, spaces, and talents associated with those experiences. These represent the assets that can be committed to supporting students in the formation of their professional identity. By inventorying the experiences carefully, and associating each experience with one or more of the competencies that the school sees as integral to its working conception of professional identity, the school can see with clarity the student's development opportunities and the functions they serve. The first job interview, for instance, might be regarded as a critical developmental moment for a student's self-direction and self-awareness competencies. A summer internship, on the other hand, might be the platform for developing a student's responsiveness and teamwork skills.

A richer picture of the pre-professional-employment period allows the law school to move to the third step – the formulation of purposeful strategies to fortify each formation experience and to unite them all in a coherent, staged, sequenced, and supported whole that maximizes the benefits for students. It may be helpful to see this as a project with two dimensions. On a more general level, relationships and collaborations need to be forged among the many people and organizations that afford students formation experiences. Lines of communication between these parties need to be opened. Ways of coordinating, enhancing, reinforcing, and leveraging their varied efforts need to be imagined and implemented. These things will not occur unless the law school takes the lead in spearheading them. On the finer level of specific strategies and actions, appraisals of the value and potential of each formation experience need to be conducted. What pedagogies can be introduced around each experience – before, during, and after it – to maximize its benefit? Who among the many, from the school's faculty and staff to stakeholders and participants outside the school, are best situated to help the student maximize that experience, and in what way may they help? What formative assessment opportunities are presented by the experience? What developmental milestones, or assessments that might later be bundled into a summative assessment, might be involved?

2.2.3 *Think about Curating and Coaching: Teaching Is Not Limited to the Transmission of Expert Knowledge*

The stereotypical law professor is a "sage on the stage" who teaches students to "think like a lawyer" by mixing masterful Socratic dialogue with wisdom and expert knowledge. Today's law professors know that the stereotype does not exhaust the pedagogic possibilities, and they should move beyond it when considering how to best support professional identity formation. Faculty who supervise students in clinical and practicum settings demonstrate the value of a "guide on the side" approach to teaching. That approach deserves the fullest exploration when supporting students in the formation of their professional identity (or, in the words of Carnegie's *Educating Lawyers*, their third apprenticeship of professional identity and sense of purpose). Framing teaching in more traditional "knowledge transmission" terms limits the options and averts our eyes from the student's experience.

What Dr. Robert Sternszus has said for medical education holds for law: "[T]he role of professional education should be to guide and support learners in the process of identity formation, rather than ensuring that learners understand medical [or legal] professionalism and demonstrate professional behaviors."[25] Students need experiences as active participants in situations that signal the profession's shared values, beliefs, and behaviors. They need encouragement to make the process of their identity formation their own and to reflect on the process as it unfolds. They need assistance in comprehending what they are going through.[26]

This calls for teachers who can curate and coach. By curating, we mean staging the experiences and environments that will promote professional identity development, connecting them conceptually to one another in an intelligently sequenced fashion, and guiding students through them with a framework that helps the students understand their own development through the process.[27] With curating, students will experience their pre-professional-employment third apprenticeship much like a well-crafted interactive exhibit that purposefully raises and reinforces themes and meanings.[28] Coaching takes the guide on the side philosophy to the personal level, meeting students where they actually happen to be and providing assistance tailored to

[25] Sternszus, *supra* note 12, at 31–32.
[26] *See* Cruess et al., *supra* note 7, at 1449 (noting that "the goals are to engage learners as active participants in the process of identity formation and to encourage them to trace their own progress through the journey"); Richard L. Cruess et al., *Introduction* to Teaching Medical Professionalism, *supra* note 10, at 1, 2–3 (noting that "[t]he role of faculty is to assist students in understanding the process of identity formation and of socialization, and to engage them in monitoring their own journey from layperson to professional," and further observing that role modeling, mentoring, experiential learning, and reflection are the educational methods most relevant to identity formation).
[27] *See* Sternszus, *supra* note 12, at 32 (noting that the cognitive base of professionalism still needs to be explicitly taught, but that the focus shifts "to providing learners with a framework with which to understand their own personal identity development").
[28] A curating approach also can help the law school assess the overall quality of the formation experiences its students receive, identify gaps and opportunities for improvement, brand and promote its formation initiatives, and explore funding from benefactors. *See* Louis D. Bilionis, *Professional Formation and the Political Economy of the American Law School*, 83 Tenn. L. Rev. 895, 905–6 (2016) (discussing curating concept).

support the next step and capitalize on its developmental potential. As Dr. Yvonne Steinert explains:

> Coaching is the thread that runs through the entire apprenticeship experi- ence and involves helping individuals while they attempt to learn or perform a task. It includes directing learner attention, providing ongoing suggestions and feedback, structuring tasks and activities, and providing additional chal- lenges or problems. Coaches explain activities in terms of the learners' understanding and background knowledge, and they provide additional directions about how, when, and why to proceed; they also identify errors, misconceptions, or faulty reasoning in learners' thinking and help to correct them. In situated learning environments, advice and guidance help students . . . to maximize use of their own cognitive resources and knowledge, an important component in becoming a professional.[29]

Consider the implications when teaching includes curating and coaching. Curating makes the third apprenticeship coherent and knowable; faculty and staff can share an understanding of professional identity formation and the school's strategy for its promotion. They then can see new possibilities for their own supportive participation in the effort. A contracts professor might turn to team-based exercises not just to spice up the teaching of doctrine and analysis but also to afford interactions that introduce the importance of collaboration when serving clients and the value to one's own development of lifelong learning through engagement with other professionals. A professor might treat a seminar discussion of contemporary policy challenges as an occasion to coach on the role that lawyers play as thought leaders in their communities. Career services counselors might take their meetings with students about job searches as coaching interactions about the fundamentals of self-direction, self-awareness, and leadership-of-self.

The centrality of curating and coaching also points the way to doing assessment right in the professional identity formation area. Everyone who coaches or observes a student in a curated experience is positioned to offer potentially valuable feedback and information. Observers inside and outside the law school can provide formative assessments to benefit students in their development along one or another competency. Those assessments can form the basis for reflection and coaching, and they can be pooled and considered collectively to mark a student's progress against milestones that reflect the stages of development envisioned for the competency.[30]

---

[29]   Steinert, *supra* note 14, at 70 (emphasis and footnote omitted).

[30]   *See* Neil Hamilton, *Professional-Identity/Professional-Formation/Professionalism Learning Outcomes: What Can We Learn About Assessment from Medical Education?* 14

In Chapter 4, we will have much more to say about student experiences that mark major transitions in a student's development, the importance of coaching and how to deliver it in the law school environment, and how to approach assessments of professional development and formation goals.

2.2.4 *Think Enterprise Wide: Professional Identity Formation Support Already Occurs throughout the Law School and Can Serve – Rather Than Detract from – Established Goals and Priorities*

When law professors contemplate their school's academic mission, they typically envision faculty as the educators and the school's administration and staff in supporting roles. That view can be limiting when it comes to supporting professional identity formation. Formation is a socialization process; students develop through interactions and activities in contexts associated with the profession and its culture.[31] Because students have professional formation experiences throughout the law school, the school's opportunities to support students in their formation run across the enterprise. No one who works at the law school lacks a potential role. Everyone can at least speak to and endorse the significance of professional identity formation in the same way that they do the values of thinking like a lawyer, doing like a lawyer, and striving for excellence. Most everyone can do more than that.

The idea that formation support is an enterprise-wide, "whole house" endeavor has significant implications. Formation-support work *already* is going on throughout the law school. Faculty do it when they lead critical inquiry in a traditional class, coach students about client counseling, teach ethics and professional responsibility classes that do not stop with the law of lawyering, require reflection exercises associated with externships, or advise students on law-reform projects in law school institutes or centers. Adjunct faculty members do it when they model how professionals strive to grow continually, achieve excellence, and serve others. When career-services counselors introduce students to the professional environments they might inhabit and coach them on how to gain entry to those worlds, they are supporting professional formation. Formation support also takes place in academic or student affairs (e.g., counseling and advising), academic support (e.g., time and stress management), and the admissions and financial aid offices (e.g., financial well-being programs).

U. St. Thomas L. J. 357, 374–88 (2018) (discussing assessment of professional formation competencies).

[31] *See supra* notes 9–17 and accompanying text.

The fact that formation work already is being done, and by so many, attests to its compatibility with a law school's mission, priorities, and people. It also signals opportunities. By thinking enterprise wide, the law school will realize that improving its support of professional formation need not mean major new investments, redistributions of resources, or reordering of priorities. It is much more about working smarter – drawing on all of the school's existing talents and resources (and tapping more outside, as alumni, practitioners, judges, government officials, the organized bar, and professional affiliation groups desire to see more attention paid to the values of professional formation and want to participate). Moreover, many features of a purposeful formation program are likely to be best practices for the pursuit of other law school goals and thus offer additional advantages to faculty and staff as well as students.

Let us pursue the point by reflecting more on the individuals who work in the law school and their varied perspectives, starting with common ground. All who work in the law school have reason to favor purposeful support of professional identity formation because it completes a holistic, professionally and morally satisfying picture of lawyer development and the school's role in that development. The school increases the probability of student success when it attends more purposefully to student competencies that are fundamental to success – such as self-awareness, leadership-of-self, self-directed learning and development, emotional intelligence, and the effective navigation of professional environments. Student success, an unqualified good, is essential to institutional success – including healthy enrollment, reputation, alumni support, and philanthropic culture. Just ask any school that has suffered misfortunes on key measures of student success in passing the bar or securing meaningful employment.

At the level of individual self-interest, faculty and staff face differing circumstances and juggle different sets of priorities under different resource conditions. All, in their own stations and situations, can find advantage in purposeful support of identity formation.

Career Services and Academic Success Professionals. Law school colleagues working in the career services area have much to gain by implementing professional identity formation initiatives in their work with students. Student success in obtaining meaningful employment is a sine qua non of success in career services, and professionals in the area believe that student "ownership" of the search for employment is a critical ingredient. What is ownership but the exercise of fundamental competencies such as self-awareness, leadership-of-self, and self-directed learning and development, along with growing cultural competency and emotional intelligence?[32] Even a rudimentary career-services office engages in coaching and counseling directed at these competencies, and some now do professional identity formation work in earnest to better position students in the competitive marketplace and contribute to their wellness and capacity for self-care in a stressful profession.[33] Professional identity formation work in career services also can strengthen and leverage relationships with the bench and the bar and align the office with the legal profession's trajectory toward competency-based professional development and evaluation.[34]

Colleagues working in the academic success area can also perceive advantages in PD&F goals. Strong bar-passage outcomes are an established goal, and competencies such as student self-directedness, resourcefulness, resilience, and self-care figure in a successful journey to licensure.[35] Initiatives to help develop those competencies are well adapted to the coaching-rich environments typically found in academic success and career-services programs. Purposeful professional identity formation work seems destined for recognition in both areas as a best practice. Such work – especially when endorsed by faculty and administration colleagues – also signals that professionals in these areas are integral and valued co-educators in the law school's program of legal education, enhancing their effectiveness and professional satisfaction.

---

[32] See Hamilton, *supra* note 24, at 594–98 (discussing "ownership" and "initiative" in relation to competencies).

[33] See Bilionis, *supra* note 28, at 904–5, 907–8 (discussing professional identity formation initiatives in the career services context and benefits to be gained). For a compendium of adoptable variants relating to the student's pursuit of employment, see Appendix A to Chapter 1.

[34] See Scott A. Westfahl & David B. Wilkins, *The Leadership Imperative: A Collaborative Approach to Professional Development in the Global Age of More for Less*, 69 Stan. L. Rev. 1667, 1716–29 (2017) (pressing the need for law firms, clients, and law schools to come into alignment with respect to the professional development of lawyers).

[35] As Professor Jerry Organ notes:

> There is some research to suggest that professional identity formation is not only not in tension with knowledge transfer and bar passage, but may be synergistically related to bar passage. The research of Larry Krieger and Ken Sheldon demonstrates that students with lower entering class credentials at one law school outperformed students with higher entering class credentials at another law school in terms of bar passage rates largely because of greater autonomy support at the law school with the lower entering class credentials.

Jerome M. Organ, *Is There Sufficient Human Resource Capacity to Support Robust Professional Identity Formation Learning Outcomes?* 14 U. St. Thomas L. J. 458, 474 (2018) (citing Kennon M. Sheldon & Lawrence S. Krieger, *Understanding the Negative Effects of Legal Education on Law Students: A Longitudinal Test of Self-Determination Theory*, 33 Personality & Soc. Psychol. Bull. 883, 891 (2007)).

Clinical Professors, Professors of Practice, Professors of Legal Research and Writing, and Externship Directors. Legal educators in clinics, practical skills courses, legal research and writing courses, and in-class components of externship programs see advantage in supporting professional identity formation. They have been doing it, if not in name, for some time now. Their educational objectives often include competencies such as teamwork and collaboration, client counseling, active listening, communication in varied contexts, giving and receiving feedback, and the management of ethical and moral tensions – building blocks of emotional intelligence, leadership, and the effective navigation of professional environments. These legal educators use guide on the side pedagogies, including coaching, feedback, and reflection. Best practices in the experiential learning and practical skills realms already feature ingredients fundamental to a program of purposeful support for professional identity formation.

Professors Teaching Doctrinal Courses. Professor Jerry Organ has depicted the situation in which professors who teach traditional doctrinal courses likely find themselves:

> Some faculty members may be inclined to move forward under the professional identity flag, but may feel like they need some help because it is a different conception of their responsibilities as professors than how they have traditionally seen themselves. . . . They may see themselves more as being engaged in "knowledge transfer" and in helping students develop critical thinking skills – the hallmarks of "first apprenticeship" teaching. But they may also appreciate that the role of the lawyer as professional is distinctive and that students would benefit from having thought more about what it means to be a lawyer while they are gaining knowledge and sharpening their analytical skills.
>
> These faculty members may require a little more direction. . . . They may need help to identity one or two concepts they could integrate into their classes without too much disruption. . . . They may need examples. . . . But with the right support, they likely will be willing to put more effort into adding professional identity formation in to their conception of their responsibilities as professors.[36]

Professors may be congenial to more purposeful formation support but uncertain of what it would entail in their own work and hence unready to proceed themselves. They need to be introduced to the possibilities and hear from peers who have positive experiences to share. One of the coauthors, Professor Bilionis, has incorporated purposeful support of professional identity

---

[36]   Organ, *supra* note 35, at 473

formation into a basic first-semester, first-year course, and the results have been gratifying. It is a constitutional law class, and students are asked to concentrate on teamwork, collaboration, and the giving and receiving of feedback – all in service of a learning outcome directed to the student's ability to "participate as a member of a professional community whose members work individually and together to continuously improve their capacities to serve clients and society."[37] While developing professional identity formation competencies, students support one another in their learning of doctrine and sharpening of analytical and critical capacities. They report that the method helps their learning, increases their confidence, and leads them to a greater appreciation of diverse viewpoints in the law. For the professor, introducing formation support explicitly establishes the student-professor relationship on broader, more satisfying ground. Empathy, trust, and support enter the picture, at no cost to analytical rigor and the transfer of knowledge. Bringing that more inclusive framework to life in the classroom invigorates the learning environment.[38]

Some professors teaching traditional subjects may conclude that their own time and talents are best focused exclusively on the cognitive and doctrinal objectives of their course. They will still have reason to support enterprise-wide efforts toward student professional identity formation, for they benefit from their students' and institution's gains. They can endorse the efforts of others and validate them for students – a practice that enthusiasts of professional formation work sometimes call "cross-selling."

Associate Deans. Associate deans with academic affairs or student affairs portfolios (we can treat them here as combined for simplicity's sake) should perceive advantage in the law school's purposeful support of professional identity formation. Their charge is to deliver a sound, competitively well-positioned program of legal education that prepares students for their futures, enriches their formative opportunities, secures their success in bar passage and employment, attends to their wellness, and meets obligations and expectations set by constituencies of consequence (including accreditors; licensing authorities; and, except for independent stand-alone schools, university leadership). The law school's collective, purposeful support of professional identity formation contributes directly to meeting that charge.

The benefits to students, faculty, and staff we have noted bear positively on the associate dean's agenda and can be consolidated into terms conducive to

---

[37] A detailed syllabus of the course and its features is available on the Holloran Center's website. See https://www.stthomas.edu/hollorancenter/roadmap/.

[38] See the discussion *infra* at Chapter 5, Section 5.7.4.

the associate dean's perspective. Law schools have a "hidden curriculum" –
acts of omission and commission within the school that can signal meanings
different from, and even at odds with, the school's formal representations.
American legal education's traditional emphasis on critical thinking and
analysis, combined with relatively slight attention to matters of professional
identity formation, has produced a hidden curriculum that privileges cognitive prowess to an extreme and to the detriment of other essential professional
attributes.[39] A purposeful, enterprise-wide formation support program coun-
teracts that hidden curriculum, placing the three apprenticeships on par with
one another and increasing the effectiveness of formation-oriented initiatives
already underway. Adding to those initiatives in purposeful ways can better
equip students to be engaged and capable learners, job seekers, and successful
takers of the bar examination. It also helps them develop resilience and
resourcefulness, valuable attributes for managing professional life. Students
can make more for themselves of law school and the opportunities and
resources it offers.

There are additional benefits for the associate dean that are less apparent to
faculty, students, and fellow administrators. When the law school establishes
purposeful support of professional identity formation as a component of its
educational program, it opens for use a new array of concepts, competencies,
and pedagogies that can help rationalize management of the curriculum and
the allocation of resources. Purposeful support of professional identity formation leads to more detailed attention to professional competencies, putting the
school on a path of alignment with competency-based education, the model
that accreditors and university leaders increasingly favor.

The Dean of the Law School. The foregoing advantages of purposeful
support of professional identity will weigh no less favorably to the dean, who
should see positive, student-centered educational reform as an answer to
a long-lingering challenge. The dean also may well appreciate the flexibility
that such an initiative affords. Significant progress can be achieved within the
framework of the traditional law school and its political economy, efficiently
and with no meaningful disturbance. Should the school adopt a competency-
based model, in whole or in part, its formation efforts will translate easily.

Thinking more broadly, the dean may recognize that reform here places the
school, as an institution, on securer footing for the present and future. How so?
A program of purposeful formation puts to fuller and more efficient use

---

[39] *See* Bilionis, *supra* note 28, at 897. For an earlier but still apt and illuminating exploration of
the hidden curriculum of the law school, and its tendency to be counterproductive to
professional identity formation, see Cramton, *supra* note 3, at 248–62.

resources already possessed by the school internally and within its reach externally. It posits that faculty and staff members are collaborators and that effective professional identity formation work is an enterprise-wide affair – thereby setting a stage where cooperation, communication, and coordination across the enterprise can be practiced constructively. It also provides a basis for integrating external stakeholders more rationally in the law school's mission. Consciously coordinated work on common ground is bound to strengthen relations that are vital to the school's success now and in years to come.

The dean also should perceive advantageous implications for the school's mission and identity. Embracing professional identity formation does not contest the importance of the first or second apprenticeships of legal education; it honors them with a galvanizing third apprenticeship. It does not question in any way the school's commitment to and investment in research; no meaningful redistribution of resources is involved, and the move has been made in medical education without adverse incident. What initiative here offers, when all is said and done, is unthreatening innovation that strengthens legal education's claim to authenticity. The American law school's mission rests on the importance to civil society of law and its practice, and the conviction that law must be the subject of disciplined academic study and effective professional training. A law school applying its best efforts to pursue that mission would adopt purposeful support of professional identity formation as a clear improvement over the status quo ante.

2.3 HOW TO ADVANCE THE LAW SCHOOL'S OWN PROFESSIONAL DEVELOPMENT

To successfully bring purposefulness to its support of students, the law school needs to be purposeful about its own development. Here are some recommendations.

2.3.1 *Support the Law School's Own Professional Development*

A lot has happened in and to American legal education in recent years. Economics and technology have begun to appreciably reshape the demand for legal services and the legal profession that provides them.[40] A major economic recession and a pandemic have made it significantly harder for students

---

[40] See, e.g., RICHARD SUSSKIND, THE END OF LAWYERS: RETHINKING THE NATURE OF LEGAL SERVICES (2008) (assessing forces that are driving change in the demand and provision of legal services).

to obtain meaningful employment, and the law school's responsibility for the success of its graduates in the employment market has heightened. Law school enrollments have declined. Competency-based education has knocked on the door in the company of accreditation reform. Distance learning has arrived.

In the matter of the third apprenticeship and professional identity formation, much has occurred as well. When we talk today about professional formation, we talk differently from how we did when *Educating Lawyers* was a fresh read. Research and thinking about how to support law students in the formation of professional identity have advanced. Medical education, meanwhile, has taken professional identity support to new frontiers, expanding the range of considerations and possibilities. New ideas, theories, themes, and vocabulary continue to enter the discussion.

To absorb it all requires claims on the law school's adaptability and capacities. The best advice to law schools is to follow the same advice they would give to a similarly situated developing lawyer: tend consciously and resourcefully to your developmental needs. Faculty and staff need to come up to speed before they can move ahead efficiently and effectively, and a plan to make that happen should be devised.[41] No school needs to reinvent the wheel. A network of educators who focus on professional formation is available to help, with the Holloran Center at the University of St. Thomas School of Law serving to grow, nurture, and support that network. The Association of American Law Schools and the National Association for Law Placement now offer programming on professional identity formation, following the lead of several organizations serving sectors and affinity groups within legal education.

2.3.2 *Be Purposeful in Project Management*

Institutions rarely have latitude to wait on change until every angle is worked out. Bringing purposefulness to a law school's support of professional formation will be its own case of stage development, with many specifications of a full-fledged program to be determined later.

The law school's project management competencies will be pressed here. The goal is a curated program that spans the pre-professional-employment period of a student's development; the challenge is to divide its creation into

---

[41] *See, e.g.*, Sylvia R. Cruess & Richard L. Cruess, *General Principles for Establishing Programs to Support Professionalism and Professional Identity at the Undergraduate and Postgraduate Levels*, in TEACHING MEDICAL PROFESSIONALISM, *supra* note 10, at 113, 116 (describing elements of a well-planned faculty development program for medical schools).

manageable projects that the school can sequence appropriately and with timely support. Some projects will stand out for fast-track work because they concern inevitable components of a solid program and represent low-hanging fruit from a resource standpoint. Enriching the career services environment to include coaching and support on self-direction, self-awareness, and leadership-of-self falls into this category. The same may be said for remodeling the school's orientation program to introduce experiences for first-year students that highlight professional identity formation as fundamental to their legal education. Revamping how the school communicates its vision of legal education – formally and in the hidden curriculum – to ensure that the third apprenticeship holds an importance equivalent to the first and second might be another early item.

A second group of projects will merit early action because an immediate leveraging opportunity presents itself. The requirement to comply with new accreditation standards, for instance, makes now the right time to establish learning outcomes linked to professional identity formation at both the law school program level and the course-specific level.

A third set of projects will feature a pace that varies with increments. These are initiatives that are advisable to begin because they are critical to the goal but involve matters about which we have much to learn – and thus warrant an iterative development process or treatment as representative experimental pilot programs.[42] Efforts to inventory the influential periods of transition that students experience, learn what makes them so, and map them to competencies might fall into this category. Devising stage development rubrics for those competencies and fashioning a comprehensive assessment model deserve similar recognition.

2.3.3 *Nurture Relationships and Collaborations*

A fully realized third apprenticeship would span the pre-professional-employment period of a student's development as a lawyer, curating experiences inside and outside the law school, enriched by coaching, reflection, and other pedagogies. Students would interact with a broad array of professionals who, in addition to aligning the environment with the legal profession, serve as role models, mentors, coaches, and providers of feedback. If the competency-based education model is adopted, formative assessments from those participants would culminate in summative assessments of the student's progress

---

[42] See Hamilton, *supra* note 30, at 399–400 (setting forth a strategy for pilot projects on competencies, stage-development models, and corresponding assessment).

against competency milestones rooted in well-conceived models of stage development. As best it can with the significantly more limited resources that it enjoys, legal education will have created its counterpart to medical education's apprenticeship of professional identity formation.

Meaningful progress toward that vision could be enough to bring about a true transformation of legal education. Pursuing that vision necessitates that the law school stretch another set of its core professional competencies – its ability to form fruitful relationships, collaborations, and teams, and to work across differences. Old hierarchies within the law school can be relaxed without fear in favor of an enterprise-wide commitment to student success that unites faculty and staff in teamwork. Old distinctions between the law school and the legal profession, between the so-called ivory tower and the so-called real world, can be transcended in favor of a vision of student development that takes place in a supportive pre-professional-employment environment where diverse stakeholders are partners in the profession. These things can happen, but only if they are pursued with conscious purpose.

2.3.4 *Understand Lessons Learned from Medical Education*

Earlier discussion in this chapter emphasized that a law school can improve its support of each student's professional identity formation and realize the benefits listed in Chapter 1 in a gradual step-by-step approach without going "all in" on competency-based education. This gradual step-by-step approach nonetheless can benefit from the lessons learned in medical education's move toward competency-based education starting in 1999, fifteen years before the ABA changed the accreditation requirements for law schools to require learning outcomes and program assessment. In the next chapter, we explore what we can learn from medical education's experience.

3

Competency-Based Education as Another Step in Purposefulness

Lessons Learned from Medical Education's Fifteen Years of Additional Experience with Professional Development and Formation Goals

The preceding chapter provided a purposefulness framework to guide a law school in realizing the four PD&F goals of helping each student to understand and internalize

- Ownership of continuous professional development toward excellence at the major competencies that clients, employers, and the legal system need;
- a deep responsibility and service orientation to others, especially the client;
- a client-centered, problem-solving approach and good judgment that ground the student's responsibility and service to the client; and
- well-being practices.

This chapter explores what legal education can learn from medical education's much more extensive experience in giving purposeful attention to the four PD&F goals. Even if a law school declines to go "all in" on competency-based education, medical education's experience provides insight into purposefulness to foster student growth on these foundational goals.

3.1 MEDICAL EDUCATION'S MOVE TOWARD DEFINING CORE COMPETENCIES AND STAGES OF DEVELOPMENT ON EACH COMPETENCY

Drs. Robert Englander and Eric Holmboe and other medical educators observe that throughout most of the twentieth century, education in the health professions and the delivery of health care services prioritized the technical expertise of the health professional and the health professions educator. Education focused on (1) a certain number of exposure hours of credit (called a "tea-steeping" model, with the student akin to a tea bag submerged in a cup of hot water for the right amount of time) and (2) academic outcomes like multiple-choice tests and licensing exams addressing technical knowledge. The student's education did not address what the licensed graduate can actually do to meet patient needs. Curricula were organized by discipline or subject and faculty-produced lessons delivered in a one-size-fits-all package of "goods" to passive learners. Little attention was paid to the learner experience.[1]

In the 1980s and 1990s, concerning signs of problems in the quality and safety of health care percolated through the health care system. By the late 1990s, the medical education community realized that it was not sufficiently preparing students to meet the challenges of a dynamic and changing health care system.[2] Medical educators came to understand that the narrow emphasis on medical knowledge and cognitive skills was inadequate to meet patient and population needs.[3] The earlier approach of "if you are really smart cognitively, you'll be fine" was not sufficient.[4] Medical educators realized the central importance of a much broader framework of patient-centered care – one that recognizes that cognitive technical skills are necessary but not sufficient to meet patient and health care system needs.[5]

By 2000, the pendulum had swung toward stronger emphasis on patient-centered care in the delivery and improvement of health care services and stronger emphasis on learner-centered and learner-driven medical education that focuses on the student's demonstration of the full range of competencies that a graduate needs to provide patient-centered care.[6] Medical educators adopted competency-based medical education (CBME) to guide this change. CBME is defined as "an outcomes-based approach to the design, implementation, assessment, and evaluation of medical education programs, using an organizing framework of competencies. A competency describes a key set of abilities required for someone to do their job."[7]

---

[1]   *See* Eric Holmboe & Robert Englander, *What Can the Legal Profession Learn from the Medical Profession About Next Steps?* 14 Univ. St. Thomas L. J. 345, 346–48 (2018); Robert Englander, Eric Holmboe et al., *Coproducing Health Professions Education: A Prerequisite to Coproducing Health Care Services*, 95 Acad. Med. 1006, 1007 (2020).

[2]   *See* Holmboe & Englander, *supra* note 1.

[3]   *Id.* at 347.

[4]   *Id.*

[5]   *Id.*

[6]   Englander & Holmboe, *supra* note 1 at 1008.

[7]   Celeste Eno, Milestone Guidebook for Residents and Fellows 2 (2020) [hereinafter Milestone Guidebook].

3.2 LESSONS LEARNED IN MOVING TOWARD COMPETENCY-BASED MEDICAL EDUCATION (CBME)

In a multistage process drawing on scholarship from education theory and medical education, fifty-nine members on an international CBME expert panel identified five core components to CBME.[8] The panel presented its vision of the five core components of CBME in a table reproduced here in Table 10.

Of the five core components in Table 10, the expert panel envisioned "Outcome Competencies" and "Sequenced Progressively" as the *central* core components guiding competency-based medical education.[9]

As Table 10 shows, medical educators started by identifying the needs of patients and the health care system. Only then could they define the critical competencies flowing from those needs that each student should develop and demonstrate.[10] With the critical competencies identified, medical educators could take the next step of sequencing the competencies, and their developmental markers, progressively.[11]

Medical educators use the term "Milestones" to describe narrative models of how student development of a core competency moves through stages toward a level of competency necessary for a licensed physician to serve clients adequately.[12] The Milestones on a specific competency provide a "shared mental model" of professional development starting as a student and progressing to competent practitioner and, beyond, to mastery.[13] A Milestone model defines a logical learning trajectory of professional development. It also highlights and makes transparent significant points in student development using a narrative that describes demonstrated student behavior at each stage.[14] Milestones can be used for formative and summative assessment as well as program assessment. If faculty and staff adopt a Milestone model for a particular competency, they also are building consensus on what competent performance looks like and thus will

---

[8]   Elaine Van Melle et al., *A Core Components Framework for Evaluating Implementation of Competency-Based Medical Education Programs*, 94 ACAD. MED. (No. 7, July 2019) at 1002–09.

[9]   *Id.*

[10] Holmboe & Englander, *supra* note 1 at 347.

[11] Holmboe and Englander note: "The next stage of evolution in the thinking of the medical education community, after defining the core competencies, was to develop a model of how the learner should proceed through a series of developmental stages in each competency. The resultant strategy was to adjust curriculum and assessment to facilitate that developmental progression." *Id.* at 350.

[12] *Id.*

[13] L. Edgar et al., *Milestones 2.0: A Step Forward*, 10 J. GRAD. MED. EDUC. 367–69 (No. 3 2018).

[14] *Id.*

TABLE 10 *The five core components of competency-based medical education*[15]

Competency-based medical education is an approach to preparing physicians for practice that is fundamentally organized around competencies derived from an analysis of patient and societal needs

CORE COMPONENTS

OUTCOME COMPETENCIES: Competencies required for practice are *clearly articulated*.	SEQUENCED PROGRESSIVELY: Competencies and their developmental markers are *sequenced* progressively.	TAILORED LEARNING EXPERIENCES: Learning experiences *facilitate the* developmental acquisition of competencies.	COMPETENCY-FOCUSED INSTRUCTION: Teaching practices *promote the* developmental acquisition of competencies.	PROGRAMMATIC ASSESSMENT: Assessment practices *support & document the* developmental acquisition of competencies.
PRACTICE: What the core component should look like in practice				
Required outcome competencies are based on a profile of graduate and/or practice-based abilities.	Competencies are organized in a way that leads to a logical developmental sequence across the continuum of medical education or practice.	Learning takes place in settings that model practice, is flexible enough to accommodate variation in individual learner needs, and is self-directed.	Teaching is individualized to the learner, based on abilities required to progress to the next stage of learning.	Learner progression is based on a systematic approach to decision-making including standards, data collection, interpretation, observation, and feedback.
PRINCIPLE: How the core component is supposed to work in practice				
Specification of learning outcomes promotes focus and accountability.	A sequential path supports the development of expertise.	Learning through real-life experiences facilitates membership into the practice community and development of competencies.	Development of competencies is stimulated when learners are supported to learn at their own pace and stage.	Programmatic assessment systems allow for valid and reliable decision-making.

[15] *Id.*

foster inter-rater reliability of assessments. Because Milestones describe what a trajectory should look like, learners can track their own progress toward becoming competent at a particular competency and programs can recognize students who are advancing well or in need of extra help.[16] Overall, each Milestone reflects the Dreyfus and Dreyfus model of development from novice to expert shown in Figure 3.

Table 11 reproduces an application of the Dreyfus model developed by the Accreditation Council for Graduate Medical Education (ACGME) to define the stages of development for patient-centered, evidence-based, and informed practice. (The reader should note that this goal or competency is similar to the third PD&F goal that we advance in this book for lawyers: a client-centered problem-solving approach and good judgment that ground each student's responsibility and service to the client.)

The ACGME developed a Milestone Model for Reflective Practice and Commitment to Personal Growth that is useful for legal education to emulate in modeling stage development with respect to PD&F Goal 1 – ownership of continuous professional development toward excellence at the major

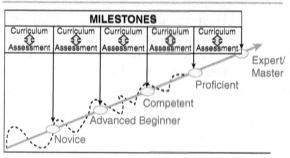

FIGURE 3 The Accreditation Council for Graduate Medical Education Milestones reflect the Dreyfus and Dreyfus model of development from novice to expert for each competency (such as the lawyer competencies shown in Figure 1). Law firms commonly call these "benchmarks."[17]

---

[16] Holmboe and Englander, *supra* note 1 at 350.

[17] P. Batalden et al., *General Competencies and Accreditation in Graduate Medical Education.*, 21 HEALTH AFF. (Millwood) 103–11 (No. 5, 2002); originally published in H. L. DREYFUS & S. E. DREYFUS, MIND OVER MACHINE: THE POWER OF HUMAN INTUITION AND EXPERTISE IN THE ERA OF THE COMPUTER (1986). Figure adapted with permission from E. Holmboe, ACGME.

TABLE 11 ACGME *harmonized milestone on evidence-based and informed practice*[18]

Stage	Characteristics of stage
1 Novice	Demonstrates how to access and use available evidence and incorporate patient preferences and values to take care of a routine patient.
2 Advanced beginner	Articulates clinical questions and elicits patient preferences and values to guide evidence-based care
3 Competent	Locates and applies the best available evidence, integrated with patient preference, to the care of complex patients
4 Proficient	Critically appraises and applies evidence even in the face of uncertainty and conflicting evidence to guide care tailored to the individual patient
5 Expert	Coaches others to critically appraise and apply evidence for complex patients and/or participates in the development of guidelines.

competencies that clients, employers, and the legal system need.[19] Similarly, the ACGME's Milestone Model on Patient-Centered Communication can be emulated with respect to PD&F Goal 2 – a deep responsibility and service orientation to others, especially the client.[20]

The Milestone and Dreyfus models contemplate that learners take ownership over their own continuous professional development to later stages on each of the competencies needed.[21] (This matches up squarely with the first PD&F goal.) Learners in a competency-based education system "must be active agents co-guiding both the curricular experiences and assessment activities."[22] What does it mean for students to be active agents in their own learning and assessment? "Learners must learn to be self-directed in seeking assessment and feedback."[23] Ideally, learners should

1. Be introduced to the overall competency-based education curriculum at the beginning and engaged in dialogue about the overall program on an ongoing basis;

---

[18] Arthur Ollendorff et al., *Harmonizing the Practice-Based Learning and Improvement Milestones*, https://www.acgme.org/Portals/0/PDFs/Milestones/HarmonizingPBLI.pdf?ver=2018-12-06-140314-100

[19] *See id.*

[20] Laura Morrison, *Harmonizing Interpersonal and Communication Skills: Assessment Through Harmonized Milestones* (2018), www.acgme.org/Portals/0/PDFs/Milestones/HarmonizingICS.pdf?ver=2018-12-06-140701-773.

[21] *See* Holmboe and Englander, *supra* note 1, at 350.

[22] *See* MILESTONE GUIDEBOOK, *supra* note 7, at 15.

[23] *Id.* at 16

2. actively seek out assessment and feedback on an ongoing basis;
3. proactively do self-assessment with feedback from external sources and reflect on both;
4. direct and perform some of their own assessments, such as seeking out direct observation of the learner by an experienced professional and creating portfolios of evidence regarding specific competencies; and
5. develop personal learning plans that are revisited and revised at least twice a year.[24]

With respect to the third core component of CBME outlined in Table 10 (tailoring learning experiences that model practice to accommodate variation in individual learner needs) and the fourth component of CBME (promoting student development by individualizing teaching based on the abilities required to progress to the next level), Table 12 explains the major differences between traditional medical education and CBME.

The change from traditional medical education to CBME began in 2000, and it is still a work in progress. Implementation has been slow, especially in

TABLE 12 A comparison of traditional versus competency-based medical education[25]

Variable	Traditional Education Model	CBME
Driving force for curriculum	Knowledge acquisition	Knowledge application
Driving force for process	Teacher	Learner
Path of learning	Hierarchal	Non-hierarchical
Responsibility of content	Teacher	Teacher and learner
Goal of educational encounter	Knowledge and skill acquisition	Knowledge and skill application
Type of assessment tool	Single assessment measure (e.g., test)	Multiple assessment measures (e.g., direct observation)
Assessment tool	Proxy	Authentic (mimics real profession)
Setting for evaluation	Removed	In clinical and professional settings
Timing of assessment	Emphasis on summative	Emphasis on formative
Program completion	Fixed time	Variable time

---

[24] *Id.*
[25] *Id.* at 2.

primary-degree schools that remain steeped in tradition and equate curriculum with exposure hours.[26] CBME is a major shift in thinking, and faculty members have lacked a shared mental model of developmental stages and standards regarding many outcomes.[27] Two decades since the shift began, medical education remains in the midst of transformation.[28]

3.3 APPLYING LESSONS LEARNED FROM CBME TO LEGAL EDUCATION

Legal education has begun its journey toward competency-based legal education (CBLE). ABA accreditation standards were revised in 2014, and by 2020, nearly all law schools in response had published learning outcomes as a first step toward CBLE. Further requirements are likely to follow. It is realistic to anticipate that the ABA as an accreditor, along with the regional accreditors for the universities with law schools, eventually will compel law schools to take the next steps beyond mere adoption of learning outcomes. If medical education's experience is any guide, legal education's movement toward CBLE will be gradual over several decades.

The good news for legal education is that the core conceptual features of a sound model of competency-based legal education are already at hand, thanks to medical education's path breaking. The structure and logic of medical education's competency-based model, depicted in Table 10 and Figure 3 earlier, are directly applicable to CBLE. Table 10's five core CBME components and Figure 3's emphasis on "Outcome Competencies" that are "Sequenced Progressively" in CBME translate easily to legal education. A competency-based legal education inspired by and modeled on CBME is depicted in Table 13 and Figure 4.

Developing a law school curriculum that employs "Outcome Competencies" that are "Sequenced Progressively" as contemplated in Table 13 and Figure 4 requires identification of the needs of clients and the legal system and then, in turn, specification of the core-competency learning outcomes that each student must develop and demonstrate to meet these needs. Work to that end is underway in legal education. The Foundational

---

[26] Englander & Holmboe, *supra* note 1, at 1008.

[27] Eric Holmboe et al., *Mastery Learning, Milestones, and Entrustable Professional Activities, in* COMPREHENSIVE HEALTHCARE SIMULATION: MASTERY LEARNING IN HEALTH PROFESSIONS EDUCATION 311, 314, 324 (W. McGaghie et al., eds., 2020).

[28] Holmboe & Englander, *supra* note 1, at 345–46.

TABLE 13 *The five core components of competency-based legal education*[29]

Competency-based legal education is an approach to preparing lawyers for practice that is fundamentally organized around competencies derived from an analysis of client and societal needs

CORE COMPONENTS				
OUTCOME COMPETENCIES: Competencies required for practice are *clearly articulated.*	**SEQUENCED PROGRESSIVELY:** Competencies and their developmental markers are *sequenced progressively.*	**TAILORED LEARNING EXPERIENCES:** Learning experiences *facilitate* the developmental acquisition of competencies.	**COMPETENCY-FOCUSED INSTRUCTION:** Teaching practices *promote* the developmental acquisition of competencies.	**PROGRAMMATIC ASSESSMENT:** Assessment practices *support and document* the developmental acquisition of competencies.
PRACTICE: What the core component should look like in practice				
Required outcome competencies are based on a profile of graduate and/or practice-based abilities.	Competencies are organized in a way that leads to a logical developmental sequence across the continuum of legal education or practice.	Learning takes place in settings that model practice, is flexible enough to accommodate variation in individual learner needs, and is self-directed.	Teaching is individualized to the learner, based on abilities required to progress to the next stage of learning.	Learner progression is based on a systematic approach to decision-making including standards, data collection, interpretation, observation, and feedback.
PRINCIPLE: How the core component is supposed to work in practice				
Specification of learning outcomes promotes focus and accountability.	A sequential path supports the development of expertise.	Learning through real-life experiences facilitates membership into the practice community and development of competencies.	Development of competencies is stimulated when learners are supported to learn at their own pace and stage.	Programmatic assessment systems allow for valid and reliable decision-making.

[29] Adapted from Table 10 *supra.*

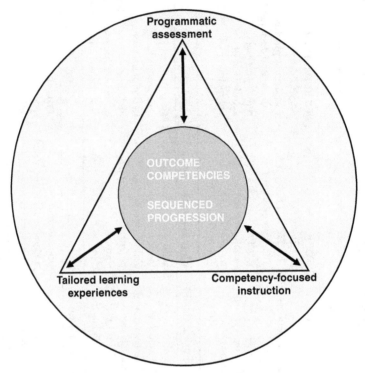

FIGURE 4 Competency-based legal education's two central core components informing the three other components in local CBLE programs[30]

Competencies Model in Figure 1 in Chapter 1 is a synthesis of the best available empirical data on the competencies that clients and legal employers need. And Figure 2 in Chapter 2 illustrates the kind of sequencing models that working groups established by the Holloran Center are devising.

In the next chapter, we will discuss ten key principles to guide legal educators who are interested in fostering student growth toward the four PD&F goals. Those principles are drawn from the five Carnegie Foundation for the Advancement of Teaching studies of higher education for the professions, CBME, scholarship on higher education generally, and moral psychology. One key take-away from CBME to carry forward into the

---

[30] Adapted from Elaine Van Melle et al., *A Core Components Framework for Evaluating Implementation of Competency-Based Medical Education Programs* 94 ACAD. MED. 1002 (2019).

TABLE 14 *The purpose and function of Milestones for the four PD&F goals*[31]

Constituency or Stakeholder	Purpose/Function
Law students	• Provide a descriptive roadmap to foster development toward later stages (new entrant students don't know what they don't know and need to be shown later stages). • Increase transparency of performance requirements • Encourage informed self-assessment and self-directed learning • Facilitate better feedback to the student • Guide personal action plans for improvement
Law schools, faculty, and staff	• Provide a meaningful framework/shared mental model of student development • Guide curriculum and assessment tool development • Provide more explicit expectations of students • Support better systems of assessment • Enhance opportunity for early identification of underperformers so as to support early intervention
ABA accreditation and the public	• Accreditation – enable continuous monitoring of programs and lengthening of site visit cycles • Public accountability – report at an aggregated national level on competency outcomes • Community of practice for evaluation and research, with a focus on continuous improvement

next chapter is that Milestone Models for PD&F goals have substantial benefits for all the major stakeholders in legal education. Table 14 outlines these benefits.

---

[31] Adapted from MILESTONES GUIDEBOOK, *supra* note 7, at 7.

4

Ten Principles to Inform Curriculum Development

In Chapter 2, we introduced a framework of purposefulness to guide law schools in their efforts to help each student understand, accept, and internalize the four PD&F goals:

- Ownership of continuous professional development toward excellence at the major competencies that clients, employers, and the legal system need;
- a deep responsibility and service orientation to others, especially the client;
- a client-centered, problem-solving approach and good judgment that ground the student's responsibility and service to the client; and
- well-being practices.

The purposefulness framework offered in Chapter 2 can assist faculty, staff, and administrators at any law school, including a school adhering to the most traditional practices of American legal education. Many signs suggest, however, that competency-based education will take hold in legal education as it has in other areas of education. We therefore set out in Chapter 3 what a purposefulness framework would look like in law schools that adopt a robust competency-based approach. Medical education already has traveled far with such an approach, and Chapter 3 drew from our peers in medicine for knowledge and practices to emulate. Importantly, those lessons and practices also can inform and shape the initiatives that law schools might take even while not subscribing to a competency-based approach.

We now turn in this and the next chapter to the practical business of doing good work in your law school. We are presupposing that our readers are faculty, staff, and administrators who want their law school to have a purposeful, effective, well-conceived, and well-developed program supporting students in the pursuit of their PD&F goals. We presuppose that progress will take time. Some schools might blueprint comprehensive initiatives at the outset, but most will proceed incrementally.

Whether one is at the drawing board devising a complete program or instead looking to create only a solid pilot project focusing on a small aspect of a select PD&F goal, *getting started and proceeding in a purposeful fashion is the most important thing.* And regardless of the scope of your particular undertaking, there are concrete principles that you can keep in mind to strengthen your work and keep it headed toward the development – in the fullness of time – of a solidly built PD&F curriculum. We see ten such principles, and they are set out in this chapter. We maintain the practical focus in Chapter 5 and draw into view the realities of trying to bring about this kind of change in the law school. We are optimistic that it can be done and offer nine practical suggestions in Chapter 5 for your consideration.

The ten principles that we will explore in this chapter are synthesized from the literature that casts light on professional identity formation and its support: (1) the five Carnegie Foundation for the Advancement of Teaching studies of higher education for the professions, (2) scholarship on higher education generally, (3) work in moral psychology, and (4) the literature on medical education's increased attention to professional identity formation.[1] For convenience, let us state all ten principles:

Principle 1 Milestone Models Are Powerful Tools
A Milestone Model can significantly strengthen efforts to support student pursuit of a PD&F goal. Work toward agreement on a model should be encouraged.

---

[1] These ten principles have been developed in a series of articles listed here. Neil Hamilton & Jerome Organ, *Thirty Reflection Questions to Help Each Law Student Find Meaningful Employment and Develop an Integrated Professional Identity (Professional Formation)*, 83 TENN. L. REV. 843, 868–75 (2016); Neil Hamilton, *Off-The-Shelf Formative Assessments to Help Each Law Student Develop Toward a Professional Formation/Professional Identity Learning Outcome of an Internalized Commitment to the Student's Own Development*, 68 MERCER L. REV. 687, 691–701 (2017); Neil Hamilton, *Formation-of-an-Ethical-Professional Identity (Professionalism) Learning Outcomes and E-Portfolio Formative Assessments*, 48 U. PAC. L. REV. 847, 856–59 (2017); Neil Hamilton, *Professional-Identity/Professional-Formation/Professionalism Learning Outcomes: What Can We Learn About Assessment From Medical Education?* 14 U. ST. THOMAS L. J. 357, 374–88 (2018) [hereinafter, *Medical Education*]; Neil Hamilton, *The Next Steps of a Formation-Of-Student-Professional-Identity Social Movement: Building Bridges Among the Three Key Stakeholders – Faculty and Staff, Students, and Legal Employers and Clients*, 14 U. ST. THOMAS L. J. 285, 299–301 (2018); Neil Hamilton & Jerome Organ, *Learning Outcomes that Law Schools Have Adopted: Seizing the Opportunity to Help Students, Clients, Legal Employers, and the Law School*, 69 J. LEGAL EDUC. (forthcoming 2021).

Principle 2 Sequenced Progressions of Curriculum and Assessment Modules Are Powerful Tools

A sequenced progression of supported experiences, with corresponding assessments, enables effective, purposeful pursuit of a PD&F goal. Work toward development of a progression should be encouraged.

Principle 3 Go Where They Are

Students are at differing developmental stages of growth on any particular goal. Each student needs to be engaged at the student's actual stage of development.

Principle 4 Reflection and Self-Assessment Are Powerful Tools

Repeated opportunities for guided reflection and guided self-assessment foster a student's growth to the next stage on any PD&F goal. Try to provide them.

Principle 5 Mentoring and Coaching Are Powerful Tools to Be Combined

Continuous one-on-one mentoring and coaching is the most effective pedagogy to foster each student's guided reflection and guided self-assessment. Try to provide it.

Principle 6 Major Transitions Are Pivotal to Development – and Major Opportunities for Support

Coaching to foster guided reflection and guided self-assessment can be especially effective at points when the student experiences a major transition on the path from being a student to being a lawyer. Pay special attention to major transitions.

Principle 7 Connect Professional Development and Formation to the Student Personally

Assist each student to see how new knowledge, skills, and capacities relating to PD&F goals are building on the student's existing knowledge, skills, and capacities and are helping the student achieve the student's postgraduation bar passage and meaningful employment goals.

Principle 8 Think Very Differently about Assessment on PD&F Goals

Combine guided self-assessment with direct observation and multi-source feedback and assessment by faculty and staff.

Principle 9 Student Portfolios Can Help Students Progress

Consider calling upon each student to create a personal portfolio on any one of the four PD&F goals, including an individualized learning plan to develop to the next level of growth.

Principle 10   Program Assessment on PD&F Goals Becomes Clear and Manageable if Principles 1 through 9 Are Heeded and Implemented
Progress on Principles 1 through 9, and particularly on Principles 1, 2, 4, 5, 8, and 9, will substantially support program assessment as required by ABA Accreditation Standard 315.

These ten principles may seem daunting, particularly to people new to thinking about professional identity formation support. We urge you to *not* consider them rules that must be followed, or steps that must be taken. Do not let aspirations toward perfection become the enemy of the good. As you undertake your work, draw on the principles to the extent that they are helpful to you. In time and with accrued experience, the value of the principles likely will become increasingly apparent, and the principles themselves something of second nature to your thinking. *Let them guide you, not govern you.*

4.1 PRINCIPLE 1 MILESTONE MODELS ARE POWERFUL TOOLS

A Milestone Model can significantly strengthen efforts to support student pursuit of a PD&F goal. Work toward agreement on a model should be encouraged.

Efforts to support students in the development of a competency can profit greatly from a Milestone Model, as Chapter 3 explained. A principal challenge for faculty and staff with respect to the PD&F goals is that, unlike a traditional learning outcome like legal analysis, the faculty and staff do not have a clear shared understanding to define the level of competence a student must achieve and the stages of development to get there. A good Milestone Model draws the particular competency at issue and its stages of development into view, enabling more purposeful and effective work at every step by everyone involved. A law school's work toward reaching reasonable agreement on a Milestone Model on *any* PD&F goal it adopts will return immediate dividends with better realization of the goal. Longer-term dividends are in the offing too. The school can build on its experience in reaching agreement on a first Milestone Model to establish models for other PD&F goals. Simply put, a Milestone Model is a powerful tool for ensuring purposefulness.

Nearly all law schools already have taken the first step toward a Milestone Model. In keeping with ABA accreditation standards, faculty and staff must establish learning outcomes for the school. A critical next step – getting those outcomes in top shape for use in a Milestone Model – is easier than it might seem. In defining, reviewing, and revising learning outcomes for the law school, faculty and staff should keep abreast of the best empirical evidence defining the knowledge, skills, and capacities a new lawyer must develop to meet the needs of clients, legal employers, and the legal system. Appendix A to Chapter 1 has the most current data, and the Foundational Competencies Model presented in Figure 1 in Chapter 1 synthesizes all these data into a framework students can visualize and understand, structured on the four foundational PD&F goals.[2]

The next step toward a Milestone Model is to embrace the idea that a student begins development of professional competencies in law school and progresses in stages of development on these same competencies well into professional life after law school. The idea is well depicted in Figure 5, which shows the competency alignment model that the Holloran Center has developed.

In simplest terms, a Milestone Model for a particular competency details what it means for the student or lawyer to be "at" the various respective stages of development depicted in Figure 5.

From this point on, devising a Milestone Model depends greatly on the particular competency; what progressive development toward mastery of the particular competency entails; and how the student's progress through stages can be fostered, evidenced, and assessed. With stages carefully identified, the school can better consider how student movement from stage to stage can be supported with experiences, coaching, reflection, and assessment.

Note that the Milestone Model associated with any PD&F goal can be aligned well with the models that legal employers are using to assess their lawyers on the same competency. The school's learning outcomes and curriculum thus will meet employer and client needs, and students will be able to communicate their value to potential employers using the employers' language.

What might Milestone Models for each of the four PD&F goals look like? Examples are presented and explained in Appendix B. We encourage readers to examine them. They will give the reader a good sense of what Milestones can look like in legal education. They can be followed or adapted and can serve as inspiration for other models. Even if your school is not ready to take

---

[2]   Schools may wish to consider an alternative synthesized framework as well. The Institute for the Advancement of the American Legal System, based on its 2016 study of 24,137 lawyers' responses to the question of what competencies are "necessary in the short term" for law graduates, has synthesized five learning outcomes. IAALS, FOUNDATIONS INSTRUCTIONAL DESIGN GUIDE (2021), https://iaals.du.edu/sites/default/files/documents/publications/founda tions_instructional_design_guide.pdf [hereinafter IAALS INSTRUCTIONAL DESIGN GUIDE]. The IAALS INSTRUCTIONAL DESIGN GUIDE also emphasizes the importance of developing clear and unambiguous definitions and descriptions for each learning outcome and each competency. *Id.* at 7, 18–20.

During Law School

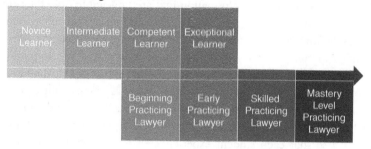

After Law School

FIGURE 5 Holloran competency alignment model showing the stages of development of learning outcome competencies: A continuum from entry into law school throughout a career[3]

such steps, familiarity with these examples can help inform and advance discussions within the law school about how to best support and assess student development.

4.2 PRINCIPLE 2 SEQUENCED PROGRESSIONS OF CURRICULUM AND ASSESSMENT MODULES ARE POWERFUL TOOLS

A sequenced progression of supported experiences, with corresponding assessments, enables effective, purposeful pursuit of a PD&F goal. Work toward development of a progression should be encouraged.

Milestone Models make clear that each student is going to be at a novice, intermediate, competent, or exceptional learner stage on a particular PD&F goal. The law school's faculty and staff want to help each student grow to the next stage of development. Suppose the PD&F goal at issue is one that the school has set as an institutional learning outcome – more than 30 percent of all law schools, for example, have adopted an institutional learning outcome on self-directed learning. Efficient and effective support for the student's

---

[3] This continuum/alignment model, developed by Neil Hamilton and Jerry Organ, builds on the Dreyfus and Dreyfus Model of development from novice to expert. *See generally* Stuart Dreyfus, *The Five-Stage Model of Adult Skill Acquisition*, 24 BULL. SCIENCE, TECH. & SOC. 177–81 (No. 3, 2004). In the model depicted in Figure 5, a "competent learner" is ready to take the bar examination and begin the practice of law after passing the exam.

progress means offering the experiences, coaching, feedback, opportunities for reflection, knowledge, and information that are targeted to help the student progress to each successive stage. Well-conceived curriculum and assessment modules do just that. Devising good modules requires a wide-angle view of the student's experiences, as many important steps in a student's formation of professional identity occur outside the traditional classroom curriculum – in cocurricular and extracurricular activities, in engagements with career services, and in summer and other outside experiences. Faculty and staff should work together as co-educators in a whole building approach as outlined in Chapter 2 so that each student experiences a sequenced and coordinated progression of curriculum and assessment modules that foster the student's growth to the next stage. In our example, faculty and staff might coordinate their efforts over time to build curriculum modules – identified experiences and the supporting pedagogy and assessment modules focusing on self-directed learning throughout the three years of law school.

A way to begin is by mapping the existing required curriculum to identify modules that currently offer experiences that foster (and assess, or could assess) student growth regarding the goal. Are the modules coordinated and building on each other? Are there gaps in a logical sequence of modules to foster each student's growth? Over time, adjustments and additions can be made to develop a coordinated progression with no significant gaps.

It is important to note that while each competency has its own stages of development, the competencies also build on one another. Some competencies form the building blocks for the development of other competencies. Figure 2 in Chapter 2 outlines this progression of competencies. Figure 2 provides guidance on how to structure a curriculum to foster each student's competencies in Group 1, then Group 2, then Group 3, then Group 4, and then Group 5. To be sure, flexibility and creativity will be rewarded in this work, and efficiencies can be captured. Because competencies build on one another, more than one competency can be the focus of a particular module.

4.3 PRINCIPLE 3 GO WHERE THEY ARE

Students are at differing developmental stages of growth on any particular goal. Each student needs to be engaged at the student's actual stage of development.

Considering each student's developmental stage on a particular competency and engaging the student at the appropriate stage are emphasized in the

Carnegie studies of higher education in the profession,[4] scholarship on moral psychology,[5] scholarship on how learning works in higher education,[6] and scholarship on medical education.[7] We emphasized the same point when setting out the core components of competency-based legal education in the preceding chapter (Table 13 in Chapter 3). Teaching must be individualized to the learner, based on the abilities required to progress to the next stage of learning.

The authors and others have been experimenting with teaching to help students toward PD&F goals in both the elective and the required curriculum for many years. Elective courses on these goals draw "the choir" from the student body who are very interested in personal and professional growth toward later stages of development on these outcomes. Designing elective PD&F courses is challenging, but the authors have had outstanding favorable student responses to these courses.

Designing a *required* PD&F course is far more challenging because students present a much broader spectrum of developmental stages. Keeping with our previous example of a school that is focusing on the goal of self-directed learning, for instance, earlier-stage students on self-directed learning tend to be passive and are unlikely to take courses that create cognitive dissonance around ownership of professional development or the integration of responsibility to others. A school that sets self-directed learning as an institutional learning outcome sensibly will conclude that a required course is necessary to reach these early-stage students. The authors' experience, however, is that instructors who intentionally create cognitive dissonance in a required course to foster growth toward PD&F goals are going to get some student pushback.

The breakthrough thinking in recent years has been to "go where they are." This means designing curriculum that reflects stage-appropriate engagement for each student. Experimentation is required, packaged and delivered with a great deal of humility, and followed by responsive adjustments. A common mistake has been to create engagements that appeal to students at later stages of development but do not appeal to earlier-stage students. This can be the case, for instance, when mentoring is employed. Mentoring a student on PD&F goals can be very powerful, and later-stage students tend to utilize mentoring well. Earlier-stage students, however, stay too passive to benefit as

---

[4] *See* Hamilton & Organ, *Thirty Reflection Questions, supra* note 1, at 868.
[5] *See id.* at 869.
[6] *See id.* at 870.
[7] *See id.* at 871.

greatly from the mentoring. Experience suggests that one-on-one coaching in the required curriculum is more effective for these more passive students than mentoring alone – a point explored further in Principle 5.

The principle of "going where they are" has further valuable implications, pointing the way to how to encourage greater student engagement with all their PD&F goals and the school's efforts to support their development. The experience of the authors suggests that many students in required courses need much more help than expected "to connect the dots" – to see the relationships between their goal of meaningful employment, the competencies that legal employers and clients want, the faculty's PD&F goals set in learning outcomes, and the actual curriculum. One study, for example, reports that 50 percent to 60 percent of the first-year and second-year students surveyed were self-assessing at one of the two earlier stages of self-directed learning.[8] Many also may need much more help in creating a narrative of strong competencies that legal employers and clients want. The enlightened interest of the student marks an entry point for the law school's PD&F support work. The curriculum should help each student understand clearly how progressing in the development of PD&F goals will help the student attain the goal of meaningful postgraduation employment – and how the curriculum and assessment modules employed by the school serve that end each step of the way. Discussion in Chapter 5 will address how to build bridges that connect PD&F goals and their curriculum and assessments to the enlightened self-interest of students, and other stakeholders as well.

4.4 PRINCIPLE 4 REFLECTION AND SELF-ASSESSMENT ARE POWERFUL TOOLS

Repeated opportunities for guided reflection and guided self-assessment foster a student's growth to the next stage on any PD&F goal. Try to provide them.

The five Carnegie studies of higher education for the professions call out the importance of "fostering each student's habit of actively seeking feedback, dialogue on the tough ethical calls, and reflection."[9] Scholarship in moral psychology also emphasizes fostering each student's reflective judgment and providing repeated opportunities for reflective self-assessment through the

---

[8] See Larry Natt Gantt II & Benjamin Madison III, *Self-Directedness and Professional Formation: Two Critical Concepts in Legal Education*, 14 U. St. Thomas L. J. 498, 504–08 (2018).

[9] See Hamilton & Organ, *Thirty Reflection Questions*, *supra* note 1, at 868.

curriculum.[10] The professionalism award winners in the Minnesota bar in Neil Hamilton and Verna Monson's study of exemplary lawyers emphasized the importance of the habit of ongoing reflection and learning in their career-long development toward later stages of all four PD&F goals.[11] Medical education research similarly underscores the importance of fostering each student's habit of reflection on experiences.[12] The Council of the ABA Section of Legal Education and Admissions recent revisions to Standard 303 emphasize that "[b]ecause developing a professional identity requires reflection and growth over time, students should have frequent opportunities during each year of law school and in a variety of courses and co-curricular and professional development activities."[13]

Reflection and self-assessment are powerful tools that should figure prominently in a student's development through the stages of any PD&F goal. Indeed, the competency to reflect and self-assess is itself a foundational professional skill, as illustrated in Tables 19 and 20 in Appendix B. There the reader will find Milestone Models for each of the first two PD&F goals. Both include the foundational sub-competency of reflection. In assessing, for instance, a student's development toward Goal 1 – ownership over the student's continuous professional development (self-directedness) – the model calls for assessing whether the student "seeks experiences to develop competencies and meet articulated goals and seeks and incorporates feedback received during the experiences" and "uses reflective practice to reflect on performance, contemplate lessons learned, identify how to apply lessons learned to improve in the future, and applies those lessons."

Defining the sub-competencies of reflection is challenging because it is a complex construct and there has been a lack of consensus on its definition.[14] The strongest definition in a professional context comes from medical education in a paper authored by Dr. Quoc Nguyen and others.[15] It is helpful to introduce that definition here to illustrate how to begin thinking about supporting reflection and self-assessment. Based on a systematic review of

---

[10]   *See id.* at 869.

[11]   Neil Hamilton & Verna Monson, *Ethical Professional (Trans)Formation: Themes from Interviews About Professionalism with Exemplary Lawyers*, 52 SANTA CLARA L. REV. 921, 949, 957 (2012).

[12]   *See Medical Education, supra* note 1, at 381.

[13]   *Interpretation* 303-5, https://www.americanbar.org/content/dam/aba/images/news/2022/02/mid year-hod-resolutions/300.pdf.

[14]   *See* Jane Uygur et al., *A Best Evidence in Medical Education Systemic Review to Determine the Most Effective Teaching Methods That Develop Reflection in Medical Students*, 41 MED. TEACH. 3 (No. 1, 2019) (calling out that the Nguyen definition is the strongest).

[15]   *See id.*

the most cited papers on reflection in the period 2008 to 2012, the authors defined reflection as "the process of engaging the self in attentive, critical, exploratory, and iterative interactions with one's thoughts and actions, and their underlying conceptual frame, with a view to changing them."[16] This conceptual model of reflection has two extrinsic elements[17] and four core sub-competencies.[18] The first extrinsic element is an experience that triggers a reflective thinking process.[19] The second extrinsic element is the timing of the reflection. In the vast majority of definitions of reflection, the timing occurs after the experience, but Nguyen and coauthors believe reflection should occur before, during, and after the experience.[20]

The four core sub-competencies (or steps) of a reflective thinking process are (1) to identify specific thoughts and actions the person is thinking about; (2) to think about the thoughts and actions attentively and critically, in an exploratory and iterative fashion; (3) to become aware of the conscious or unconscious conceptual framework(s) that underlie the person's thoughts and actions; and (4) to have a purpose of changing the self in terms of the person's conscious or unconscious conceptual framework.[21] The curriculum should provide multiple opportunities for students to develop the habit of engaging in this reflective thinking process.[22] Appendix D for Chapter 4, has both a Milestone Model on the competency of reflection and a Milestone Model to grade an individual reflection assignment.

Students benefit greatly from coaching to guide this reflective thinking process. The findings of a meta-study of empirical research on teaching interactions in medical education emphasizes that "it is important for students to receive some assistance in navigating the complexity of reflection, and students benefit from learning about reflection through introductions, guidelines to writing, and receiving feedback on their work."[23] The literature also points to the role of a mentor/coach as essential for scaffolding medical

---

[16]   Quoc D. Nguyen et al., *What Is Reflection? A Conceptual Analysis of Major Definitions and a Proposal for a Five-Component Model*, 48 Med. Educ. 1176, 1182 (2014).

[17]   *See id.* at 1184.

[18]   *See id.* at 1182. Nguyen et al. include a fifth core sub-competency called "having a view on the change itself" that picks up the continuing process of how an envisioned change can be changed further with a continuing process of reflection. *Id.* To keep the model proposed here simpler, this fifth sub-competency is not included.

[19]   *Id.* at 1184.

[20]   *Id.*

[21]   *Id.* at 1181–82.

[22]   *See Medical Education, supra* note 1, at 381.

[23]   *See* Uyger et al., *supra* note 14, at 13.

students' reflections.[24] We turn to the importance of mentoring and coaching next, as it is embraced in our fifth principle.

4.5 PRINCIPLE 5 MENTORING AND COACHING ARE POWERFUL TOOLS TO BE COMBINED

Continuous one-on-one mentoring and coaching is the most effective pedagogy to foster each student's guided reflection and guided self-assessment. Try to provide it.[25]

Guided reflection and guided self-assessment are critical contributors to a student's successful progressive growth on any PD&F goal. The growth process will entail numerous experiences – including professionally authentic experiences that can be particularly valuable – occurring in a coordinated sequence of modules that rationalize the student's stage development toward the goal. What pedagogy best supports the student's guided reflection and guided self-assessment throughout that progression? A one-on-one continuous mentoring/coaching model stands out as most conducive to effective support. This model affords additional benefits that law school faculty and staff will find attractive; we will address those benefits later. First, we will explore what the literature tells us about mentoring and coaching. Many who enter the work of supporting law student professional-identity formation will take on the role of a mentor or coach, perhaps even without knowing it. Awareness of what it means to take on those roles, and to do them well, will prove useful. An individualized one-on-one continuous mentoring/coaching model to provide guided student reflection and assessment is supported by leading scholars. Ida Abbott, a scholar on mentoring in the legal profession, points out that the lines between mentoring and coaching are fluid because both roles "provide individualized and personal support by a trusted advisor."[26] She also notes that "[a]s coaching becomes more popular, boundaries between mentoring and coaching will blur and overlap."[27] Regarding mentoring, earlier scholarly literature spoke of a "career mentoring function" that directly aided the

---

[24]　Salah E. Kassab et al., *Construct Validity of an Instrument for Assessment of Reflective Writing-Based Portfolios of Medical Students*, 11 ADV. MED. EDUC. PRACT. 397, 399 (2020).

[25]　This discussion of Principle 5 is taken from a forthcoming article. *See* Neil Hamilton, *Mentor/ Coach: The Most Effective Curriculum to Foster Each Student's Professional Development and Formation*, 17 U. ST. THOMAS L. J. (forthcoming 2022) (available at http://ssrn.com/abstract=3747309).

[26]　IDA ABBOTT, THE LAWYER'S GUIDE TO MENTORING 41 (2d ed. 2018).

[27]　*Id.* at 38.

protégé's career advancement.[28] Taking a historical perspective, Abbott has defined mentoring to be "a relationship-based process that helps individuals learn, grow and achieve high levels of professional success and fulfillment,"[29] adding "[m]entoring occurs when a more experienced and trusted lawyer takes an interest in an individual's career development and success."[30] Mentors have relevant work and career experience, provide career and psychological support, and can create or directly affect career-enhancing opportunities.[31]

Regarding coaching, Abbott explains that coaches help individuals "uncover personal and professional goals, develop a plan to achieve those goals, and provide ongoing support while the plan is implemented."[32] Coaches are trained to "listen, ask powerful questions, serve as a sounding board, motivate and hold accountable the people they work with";[33] "[c]oaches do not need to be lawyers (although they often are) because coaching employs a process where they are not offering advice or conveying substantive information."[34] Coaches help lawyers create plans and develop strategies for career advancement.[35] In Abbott's analysis, "[a] major advantage that mentors have over coaches in law firms concerns career advancement."[36] Abbott compares mentoring and coaching in Table 15.

John Whitmore, author of the first book on workplace coaching,[37] defines coaching as "unlocking people's potential to increase their own performance. It is helping them to learn rather than teaching them."[38] Coaching supports people "to clarify their purpose and vision, achieve their goals, and reach their potential."[39] Whitmore believes mentoring is more about sharing expertise and passing down knowledge with some guidance.[40]

Coaching focuses on developing a student's self-understanding and discernment of purpose, vision, and goals, and the student's self-direction as manifested in the creation and implementation of a plan to achieve the student's

---

[28]   Neil Hamilton & Lisa Brabbit, *Fostering Professionalism Through Mentoring*, 57 J. LEGAL EDUC. 102, 107 (2007).

[29]   Ida Abbott consulting website. (Last visited August 10, 2020, https://idaabbott.com/mentoring/).

[30]   IDA ABBOTT, LAWYER'S PROFESSIONAL DEVELOPMENT 212 (2012).

[31]   Abbott, *supra* note 26, at 42–43.

[32]   *Id.* at 42.

[33]   *Id.*

[34]   *Id.* at 42–43.

[35]   *Id.* at 43.

[36]   *Id.* at 44.

[37]   JOHN WHITMORE, COACHING FOR PERFORMANCE 1 (5th ed., 2017).

[38]   *Id.* at 248.

[39]   *Id.*

[40]   *Id.* at 14, 249.

TABLE 15 *Comparison of mentors and coaches*[41]

	Mentor	Coach
Primary function	Career support, psychological support	Goal achievement, performance
Focus	Professional development	Functional improvement, results
Audience	All lawyers	High-potential and under-performing lawyers
Attributes	Willing/able to model, advise, support, transfer knowledge	Trained in coaching techniques
Level of intensity	Moderate	Moderate
Level of trust required	Moderate–high	Moderate

vision and goals. Mentoring emphasizes relationship-based career support for students by mentors with relevant work and career experience who use their own experience, insight, and advice to help mentees learn and progress.

Consideration of two of our PD&F goals will illustrate the value of coaching *and* mentoring. To grow to the next level of the first PD&F goal – ownership of continuous professional development toward excellence at the major competencies that clients, employers, and the legal system need – a student needs coaching situated in the context of the student's own path in the legal market and the student's own development. The student also needs mentoring that helps the student become more familiar with the legal market and how to navigate within it toward success in a career. To grow to the next level of the second PD&F goal – a deep responsibility and service orientation to others, especially the client – a student needs mentoring that illuminates how professional skills are used to forge and maintain relationships with clients that serve the clients' needs. Yet each student also needs coaching to develop and implement a plan to achieve the needed growth to the next level.

Abbott emphasizes that mentors must themselves have proven legal skills and ownership over continuous professional development to be effective.[42] Mentors facilitate a mentee's learning by helping mentees process what they are observing and experiencing and then apply what the mentees have learned to different circumstances.[43] Mentors actively listen to their mentees, show

---

[41] Abbott, *supra* note 26, at 42.
[42] *Id.* at 94.
[43] *Id.*

empathy,[44] and give meaningful feedback.[45] They build mentee confidence[46] and counsel on career development and career advancement issues.[47]

Workplace coaching is still an emerging profession.[48] There is very little legal scholarship on coaching[49] even though larger law firms are increasingly using coaching to help individual lawyers learn specific professional skills.[50] There is, however, some scholarship about the most important competencies for professional coaching generally. The International Coaching Federation (ICF) has accredited more than 30,000 professional coaches worldwide.[51] ICF released an updated Coaching Core Competencies Model in October 2019 based on evidence collected from more than 1,300 professional coaches.[52] The ICF identifies eight core professional coach competencies. The professional coach

1. Demonstrates ethical practice including confidentiality;
2. embodies a coaching mindset including ongoing reflective practice and ongoing development as a coach;
3. establishes and maintains clear agreements for the overall coaching engagement with the client;
4. cultivates trust and safety with the client including understanding and respecting the client's context and identity and support, empathy, and concern for the client;
5. maintains presence including being fully present with and responsive to the client;
6. listens actively;
7. evokes client awareness, insight, and learning by using tools such as powerful questioning, silence, metaphor, or analogy; and

---

[44]   *Id.* at 99.
[45]   *Id.* at 94–95.
[46]   *Id.* at 96–97.
[47]   *Id.* at 99.
[48]   E. de Haan, *A Systematic Review of Qualitative Studies in Workplace and Executive Coaching: The Emergence of a Body of Research*, 71 CONSULTING PSYCH. J.: PRAC. & RSCH. 227, 228 (2019), https://doi.org/10.1037/cpb0000144.
[49]   One recent article has addressed the issue. *See* Susan R. Jones, *The Case for Leadership Coaching in Law Schools: A New Way to Support Professional Identity Formation*, 48 HOFSTRA L. REV. (2020) (advocating coaching to foster law student leadership skills).
[50]   Nicholas Jelfs-Jelf, *How Are Law Firms Using Coaching?*, https://www.linkedin.com/pulse/how-law-firms-using-coaching-nicholas-jelfs-jelf/ (noting a survey of Am Law 200 firms where 123 firms reported they are using coaching).
[51]   *International Coaching Federation*, https://en.wikipedia.org/wiki/International_Coaching_Federation.
[52]   *Updated ICF Core Competencies*, Oct. 2019, https://coachfederation.org/app/uploads/2020/07/RevisedCompetencyModel_July2020.pdf .

8. facilitates client growth by transforming learning and insight into goals and action.[53]

John Whitmore's model of workplace coaching, advanced in his ground-breaking book now in its fifth edition, has been influential. Whitmore argues that "by and large, [coaches] subscribe to a common set of principles."[54] He lists three fundamental skills of coaching:

1. Asking powerful open questions to raise the coachee's awareness and responsibility.[55]
   a. "Awareness" includes:
      (i) awareness of self – understanding why you do what you do;
      (ii) awareness of others – knowing other people's strengths, interferences, and motivations; and
      (iii) awareness of the organization – aligning individual, team, and organizational goals.[56]
   b. "Responsibility" is taking ownership of the coachee's own development and high performance, and committing to action.[57]
2. Listening well.[58] Whitmore defines listening well as active listening and includes a table of active listening sub-competencies.[59]
3. Following the GROW model with respect to the sequence of questions.[60]
   – Goal-setting for the session as well as the short and long term (What do you want?);
   – Reality checking to explore the current situation (Where are you now? And what blocks your path?);
   – Options and alternative strategies or courses of action (What could you do?); and
   – What is to be done, when, by whom, and the will to do it (What will you do?).[61]

---

[53] *Id.*
[54] Whitmore, *supra* note 37, at 2.
[55] *Id.* at 41–43. Whitmore includes specific powerful open questions at pages 81–88.
[56] *Id.* at 41–42.
[57] *Id.* at 252, 73.
[58] *Id.* at 43.
[59] *Id.* at 93.
[60] *Id.* at 43, 96.
[61] *Id.* at 96, 58. Goal Setting is explored further at pages 102–14; What Is Reality is explored further at page 125; What Options Do You Have is explored further at pages 126–32; What Will You Do? is explored further at page 152.

Whitmore emphasizes that the key to using the GROW model is to spend sufficient time asking questions exploring goals "until the coachee sees a goal that is both inspirational and stretching to them, and then to move flexibly through the sequence according to [the coach's] intuition, revising the goal if needed."[62] Whitmore also emphasizes asking open questions that generate awareness and responsibility. While coaching is not all about asking questions, that is the single most important skill to master for a novice coach.[63] Whitmore provides a "Coaching Question Toolkit" containing questions that experienced coaches have found consistently helpful in coaching:[64] "The golden rule is to be clear and brief. Sometimes the most powerful questions lead to a long silence so the coach should not feel the need to jump in with another question if there is a long pause."[65]

The ICF core coaching competencies, the Whitmore fundamental coaching skills, and Abbott's mentoring skills emphasize similar foundational skills. We draw from and elaborate upon them in Table 16 to offer a list of foundational competencies for the mentor/coach in the law student context.

Empirical evidence shows that coaching in a 45- to 60-minute interview to promote student reflection with respect to self-directed learning is effective and can have an important and lasting impact on a student.[66] In a study of 102 undergraduates (with a mean age of 21), a trained interviewer conducted a one-on-one in-person interview designed to promote reflection about the

TABLE 16 *Foundational competencies for a law student mentor/coach*

1. Actively listening to understand both where the student is developmentally and what are the student's goals;
2. Asking powerful open questions to foster the student's guided reflection and guided self-assessment and raise the student's awareness and responsibility;
3. Facilitating student growth toward later stages of the PD&F goals by transforming learning (especially learning in authentic professional experiences) and insight into clear and realistic goals, options, and action;[67] and
4. Understanding and respecting the student's context and identity and providing support, empathy, and concern for the student.

---

[62] *Id.* at 100.
[63] *Id.* at 254.
[64] *Id.* at 254–61.
[65] *Id.* at 254.
[66] *See* Matthew J. Bundick, *The Benefits of Reflecting on and Discussing Purpose in Life in Emerging Adulthood*, 132 NEW DIRECTIONS YOUTH DEV. 89, 93 (2011).
[67] *See* Whitmore, *supra* note 37, at 43, 96.

student's purpose in life, core values, and most important life goals. The study included a pretest and a posttest nine months later to assess the impact of the interview.[68] On average, the coaching engagement led to benefits for student goal-directedness toward life purpose nine months later.[69] The author of the study suggests that these coaching conversations are "a triggering event [that] would impel an emerging adult, who is likely in this stage of life to be predisposed to identity exploration, to reflect on life beyond the interview in considering his or her life path."[70] In general, individualizing students' learning experiences, so the student can practice rather than just observe, and combining those individualized experiences with an instructor who provides continuous feedback to the student has been associated with more learning benefits than large group training with respect to self-directed learning.[71]

The students' ultimate goals are to pass the bar and find meaningful postgraduation employment. A mentor who has relevant work and career experience will have credibility with the students regarding the students' goals. An experienced mentor/coach using the foundational competencies for law student coaching in Table 16 can foster each student's growth toward later stages of the PD&F goals while helping the students achieve their goals.

It should be clear that the mentor/coach is putting Principle 3 into action by "going where they are" and engaging each student at the student's present developmental stage. The mentor/coach is also observing Principle 4 by providing repeated opportunities, particularly at major transitions as discussed in the next principle, for guided reflection and guided self-assessment to foster each student's growth to the next stage of a PD&F goal. The mentor/coach can help each student with self-assessment on the relevant Milestone Model for a particular learning outcome (contributing to fulfillment of Principle 1) and provide outside observer assessment concerning a student's stage of development. The mentor coach can help each student create and implement a plan to move through a coordinated progression of modules to foster the student's growth to the next level (contributing to fulfillment of Principle 2).

At the outset of our discussion of this principle, we noted that a model of synthesized mentoring and coaching offers additional benefits to the law school and its students. Many law schools today are undertaking diversity, equity, and inclusion (DEI) initiatives and student well-being initiatives. Positive student experiences with coaches and mentors can contribute to the goals of those

---

[68] Bundick, *supra* note 66, at 93.

[69] *Id.* at 97–98.

[70] *Id.* at 98.

[71] *See* Ryan Brydges et al., *Self-Regulated Learning in Simulation-Based Training: A Systematic Review and Meta-Analysis*, 49 MED. EDUC. 368, 369–70, 372, 374 (2015).

initiatives. Recent empirical research on student well-being and DEI emphasizes the importance of "psychologically attuned interventions [that] emphasize
a person-by-situation approach that is neither person-centric nor fully context-
centric. In this approach, personal factors (e.g., law student social identities,
such as race, gender, or social class) interact with societal stereotypes and
environmental cues to shape thoughts, feelings, and behavior."[72] The aim of
these psychologically attuned interventions is to alter people's process of making
meaning and sense about themselves to change the interactions between people
and contexts over time.[73] For example, "social-belonging interventions facilitate
beliefs that may help students' sense of belonging and psychological safety in the
face of challenges."[74] Growth mindset interventions change people's process of
making meaning with respect to one's own and others' abilities and potential to
grow.[75] Individualized coaching will also foster student performance and well-
being. Self-Determination Theory research shows that providing autonomy
support to students where the teacher conveys understanding of the student
and provides the student with choices increases the student's ability to perform
maximally, to fulfill psychological needs, and to experience well-being.[76]

4.6 PRINCIPLE 6 MAJOR TRANSITIONS ARE PIVOTAL TO DEVELOPMENT – AND MAJOR OPPORTUNITIES FOR SUPPORT

*Coaching to foster guided reflection and guided self-assessment can be especially
effective at points when the student experiences a major transition on the path
from being a student to being a lawyer. Pay special attention to major
transitions.*

Fostering each student's guided reflection particularly at major transitions
during law school is very important.[77] Each law student experiences significant transitions where the student is growing, step by step, from being a novice

---

[72]   Victor D. Quintanilla & Sam Erman, *Mindsets in Legal Education*, 69 J. LEGAL EDUC. 412, 431 (2020).

[73]   *Id.* at 433. The article explains the particular vulnerabilities of students from disadvantaged groups regarding social belonging at pages 422–25.

[74]   *Id.* at 435.

[75]   *Id.*, at 425–27.

[76]   Lawrence S. Krieger & Kennon M. Sheldon, *What Makes Lawyers Happy?: A Data-Driven Prescription to Redefine Professional Success*, 83 GEO. WASH. L. REV. 554, 582 (2015).

[77]   Some of the discussion here on Principle 6 is taken from Neil Hamilton, *The Major Transitions in Professional Formation and Development from Being a Student to Being a Lawyer Present Opportunities to Benefit the Students and the Law School*, 73 BAYLOR L. REV. 139 (2021).

outsider with a stance of being an observer ultimately to join a community of practice as an insider to the profession.

There is a distinction between the situational changes a law student experiences and the significant transitions of law school. During law school, each student experiences a number of situational changes like physically moving to a new city to attend law school or starting a new class or a new year of law school. A significant transition, however, is a psychological inner reorientation and self-definition that the student must go through to incorporate the situational changes into a new understanding of professional life's developmental process.[78] It is clear that the major periods of inner reorientation and self-definition for a law student are exceptional opportunities for the law faculty and staff to foster student growth toward later stages of the school's learning outcomes.

Research on medical education emphasizes that a new entrant to a profession like medicine is growing, step by step, from being an outsider with a stance of an observer to joining a new group or "community of practice" as an insider in a profession.[79] Medical professors Lockyer, de Groot, and Silver explain:

> Generally, transitions are critically intense learning periods associated with a limited time in which a major change occurs and that change results in a transformation. During transitions, people re-form their way-of-being and their identity in fundamental ways. Thus, transitions represent a process which involves a fundamental reexamination of one's self, even if the processing occurs at a largely unconscious level. In transition periods, people enter into new groups or "communities of practice." This involves adopting shared, tacit understandings, developing competence in the skilled pursuit of the practice, and assuming a common outlook on the nature of the work and its context.[80]

---

[78] WILLIAM BRIDGES, TRANSITIONS: MAKING SENSE OF LIFE'S CHANGES xii, 81, 105–75 (2d ed. 2004).

[79] *See* Louis D. Bilionis, *Bringing Purposefulness to the American Law School's Support of Professional Identity Formation*, 14 U. ST. THOMAS L. J. 480, 484 (2018) (citing William M. Sullivan, *Foreword* to TEACHING MEDICAL PROFESSIONALISM: SUPPORTING THE DEVELOPMENT OF A PROFESSIONAL IDENTITY ix, xii (Richard L. Cruess et al. eds., 2d ed. 2016) [hereinafter TEACHING MEDICAL PROFESSIONALISM]).

[80] Jocelyn Lockyer et al., *Professional Identity Formation: The Practicing Physician, and Continuing Professional Development, in* TEACHING MEDICAL PROFESSIONALISM *supra* note 79, at 186, 188. Dr. Robert Sternszus notes that "[p]rofessional identity results from a series of identity transformations that occur primarily during period of transition." Robert Sternszus, *Developing a Professional Identity: A Learner's Perspective, in id.* at 26, 31.

These transitions are often characterized by anxiety, stress, and risk for the developing professional.[81] As medical professor Sternszus observes, "The literature supports the notion that transitions in medical education are both highly stressful and inadequately supported."[82]

A 2018 meta-analysis reviewed seventy articles on medical transitions to synthesize the evidence and provide guidance for medical education.[83] The focus on transitions and their importance is apparent. The authors found that the strongest empirical evidence asked medical faculties

1. To provide learning opportunities at transitions that include authentic (real-life or mimicking real-life) professional experiences that build progressively toward an understanding of principles. The authenticity of the learning becomes increasingly important as the learners become more independent.[84]

Moderate to strong recommendations (i.e., supported by solid evidence from one or more papers plus the consensus of the authors of the article) were for medical faculties

2. To encourage progressive incremental independence by offering a sliding scale of decreasing supervision alongside demonstrating increasing trust in the student;[85]

3. to apply concepts of graduated responsibility to nonclinical as well as clinical domains of training, such as leadership and responsibility;[86]

4. to make trainees aware of the psychological impact of actual responsibility including the process of their own professional formation as they move up each level of training;[87]

---

[81] Richard L. Cruess et al., *Reframing Medical Education to Support Professional Identity Formation*, 89 ACAD. MED. 1146, 1147 (2014); Sternszus, *supra* note 80, at 33 ("Transitions represent some of the most challenging times for medical trainees."); Lynn V. Monrouxe, *Theoretical Insights into the Nature and Nurture of Professional Identities*, in TEACHING MEDICAL PROFESSIONALISM, *supra* note 79, at 37, 43.

[82] Sternszus, *supra* note 80, at 30.

[83] S. Yardley et al., *The Do's, Don't and Don't Knows of Supporting Transition to More Independent Practice*, 7 PERSP. MED EDUC. 8 (2018).

[84] *Id.* at 14. A study of the University of New Hampshire Law School's Daniel Webster Scholars Program concluded that two factors drive the accelerated development of competencies by the students in the program: (1) contexts that simulated practice and (2) opportunities for reflection and formative assessment. *See* INSTITUTE FOR THE ADVANCEMENT OF THE AMERICAN LEGAL SYSTEM, AHEAD OF THE CURVE: TURNING LAW STUDENTS INTO LAWYERS 14, 24 (2015), https://iaals.du.edu/publications/ahead-curve-turning-law-students-lawyers.

[85] Yardly, *supra* note 83, at 17–18.

[86] *Id.* at 18.

[87] *Id.*

5. to establish a mentorship program with local champions to provide feedback to develop learners' competence and confidence (supported reflection and discussion are important in the process of becoming an independent practitioner);[88] and

6. to seek to aid the development of resilience and independence.[89]

How do law students themselves assess the important transitions in their journey from novice to competent learner/beginning practicing lawyer with respect to PD&F goals? To start answering this question, coauthor Professor Hamilton developed a Qualtrics survey for law students at the University of St. Thomas School of Law in September of the 2L year asking them to reflect on the transitions of the 1L year and the summer between the 1L and the 2L years.[90] The survey focused on transitions regarding ownership over continuous professional development (the stages are set forth in Table 19 in Appendix B). At St. Thomas, all 2Ls take Professional Responsibility in the 2L year, and sixty-two of the sixty-two students present in Hamilton's Professional Responsibility class on September 6, 2018, filled out the survey. The survey question was: "In the context of the self-directed learning stage development model [in Table 19], what is the impact of each experience in this survey on your transition from thinking and acting like a student to thinking and acting like a junior lawyer?" The respondent could choose among the following: no impact, some impact, moderate impact, substantial impact, and great impact. There also was an opportunity for respondents to add additional experiences that were significant with respect to the survey question, but none of the added experiences was mentioned by more than a single respondent. Table 17 indicates the experiences that had the greatest impact.

Table 17 makes clear that 2L students reflecting on the major transitions in the 1L year and the summer following the 1L year rate professionally authentic experiences (those that are real-life or mimic the real-life work of a lawyer) as having the greatest impact on their growth toward later stages of ownership of their own continuous professional development. A very high proportion of students rated their most impactful experience in summer employment (59 percent) and paid or unpaid summer employment generally (52 percent) as having a great impact on their transition from thinking and acting like a student to thinking and acting like a junior lawyer. The third most impactful

---

[88] *Id.* at 19–20.

[89] *Id.* at 20.

[90] The University of St. Thomas Institutional Review Board approved of this project 1112166–1 on September 14, 2017. The survey is available at https://stthomas.az1.qualtrics.com/jfe/form/SV_4MVFsoLh9jFA4br.

TABLE 17 *Experiences in the 1L year and the following summer that 50 percent or more of the students thought had a great, substantial, or moderate impact on their transition from thinking and acting like a student to thinking and acting like a junior lawyer with respect to ownership over continuous professional development*

Other Experiences	Percentage of the Students Answering Great, Substantial, or Moderate Impact
Summer Employment: most impactful experience	89% (with 59% responding great impact)
Paid or unpaid summer employment experience	87% (with 52% responding great impact)
Receiving graded memo from Lawyering Skills	87% (with 19% responding great impact)
Final Examination Period (Fall Semester)	87% (with 16% responding great impact)
Mentor Externship: most impactful experience	85% (with 19% responding great impact)
Job Search for the Summer	82% (with 14% responding great impact)
First Week of Classes	81% (with 11% responding great impact)
Final Examination Period (Spring Semester)	77% (with 19% responding great impact)
Oral Arguments for Lawyering Skills II	76% (with 14% responding great impact)
Fall Midterms	76% (with 10% responding great impact)
First CLE/Networking Events with Lawyers	71% (with 10% responding great impact)
First Time Being Cold-Called in Class	70% (with 13% responding great impact)
Spring Midterms	67% (with 4% responding great impact)
Mentor Externship Experiences Generally	64% (with 16% responding great impact)
Spring Semester Final Grades	63% (with 27% responding great impact)
Roadmap Coaching	60% (with 9% responding great impact)
Roadmap Written Assignment	60% (with 4% responding great impact)
First Career and Professional Development (CPD) Meeting	58% (with 2% responding great impact)
Orientation	58% (with 3% responding great impact)
Fall Semester Grades	55% (with 13% responding great impact)

experience was receiving back the first graded memorandum in their lawyering skills course (with 19 percent responding great impact), and the fifth most impactful experience was in a mentored externship[91] (19 percent responding great impact). These, too, are professionally authentic experiences.

---

[91]   The University of St. Thomas School of Law has a required Mentor Externship where each student has an assigned mentor in the practicing bar in each year of law school.

Paid or unpaid summer employment experience after the 1L year is a singularly important professionally authentic transition. Summer employment is outside of the formal curriculum, but the law school can and should provide some coaching and guided reflection for each student about the summer employment transition experience. It seems far too rich an opportunity to squander.

The major takeaway from Table 17 is that law schools should provide some curricular support at several significant transitions where students may also experience substantial stress, including particularly

1. Immediately after the summer employment experience;
2. immediately after major professionally authentic experiences like the first graded memorandum or an oral argument in a lawyering skills course; and
3. immediately after students receive fall semester grades and are considering summer employment.

There is a major need for further survey research on students in all three years of law school to identify more clearly the major transitions they experience. The authors' best practical judgment on the major transitions in the 2L and 3L years is in Appendix C.

4.7 PRINCIPLE 7 CONNECT PROFESSIONAL DEVELOPMENT AND FORMATION TO THE STUDENT PERSONALLY

Assist each student to see how new knowledge, skills, and capacities relating to PD&F goals are building on the student's existing knowledge, skills, and capacities and are helping the student achieve the student's postgraduation bar passage and meaningful employment goals.

Adult learning theory emphasizes two themes that are important for faculty and staff seeking to support law students in the formation of professional identity:

(1) Students are more motivated to learn if they can see that the subjects are relevant to their goals;[92] and
(2) students learn most effectively when they are able to connect new knowledge and skills to prior knowledge and skills.[93]

---

[92] Susan Ambrose et al., How Learning Works: Seven Research-Based Principles for Smart Teaching 68–69, 74–75 (2010).
[93] *Id.* at 15–16, 33, 83.

Students will better pursue their PD&F goals if they see how those goals connect to their own abilities and aspirations, and students need assistance to see those connections. Providing that assistance will heighten engagement and strengthen learning, and that is reason enough to undertake the effort. The "hidden curriculum" features of the typical law school environment only underscore the importance of providing assistance to students. Students often interpret the strong emphasis traditionally placed on the cognitive competencies associated with "thinking like a lawyer" as a signal that competencies having to do with professional identify formation are a low priority. The signal, though unintended, is an impediment to motivation and engagement with respect to PD&F goals.

How to make the needed connection? Understanding the personal goals of law students is essential, and there are good data. The 2018 Association of American Law Schools (AALS) report, *Before the JD: Undergraduate Views on Law School*, is the first large-scale, national study to examine what factors contribute to an undergraduate student's decision to go to law school.[94] The AALS study is based on responses from 22,189 undergraduate students from twenty-five four-year institutions and 2,727 law students from forty-four law schools.[95] The survey asked the undergraduates, "How important are each of these characteristics to you when thinking about selecting a career?" The top three characteristics that undergraduate students considering law school thought were "extremely important" are

1. Potential for career advancement (selected by 62 percent of the respondents);
2. opportunities to be helpful to others or useful to society/giving back (selected by 54 percent of the respondents); and
3. ability to have a work-life balance (selected by 50 percent of the respondents).

Overall, a synthesis of the AALS data indicates the most important goal of undergraduate students considering law school is meaningful postgraduation employment with the potential for career advancement that "fits" the passion, motivating interests, and strengths of the student and offers a service career that is both helpful to others and has some work/life balance. A 2017 empirical study of enrolled 1L students in five law schools is consistent with this synthesis. The study asked, "What are the professional goals you would like to

94   ASSOCIATION OF AMERICAN LAW SCHOOLS, BEFORE THE JD: UNDERGRADUATE VIEWS ON LAW SCHOOL 43 (2018).
95   *Id.* at 5.

achieve by six months after graduation?" The two most important goals were bar passage and meaningful employment, followed by sufficient income to meet loan obligations and a satisfactory living.[96]

Drawing on twenty years of empirical research on emerging adults in the age range 18 to 29, James Arnett finds that there is a very strong American consensus that becoming an adult means becoming self-sufficient, learning to stand alone as an independent person.[97] Three criteria are at the heart of emerging adults' view of the self-sufficiency required for adulthood: (1) taking responsibility for yourself, (2) making independent decisions, and (3) becoming financially independent.[98]

The curriculum on the four PD&F goals needs repeatedly to connect the dots so that each student sees that growing to a later stage on one of these learning outcomes helps the student reach their postgraduation goals. Chapter 1 outlined these benefits. Each student will need coaching on how to communicate in the language legal employers use for these competencies. The Foundational Competencies Model in Figure 1 of Chapter 1 provides these vocabularies.

The curriculum on the four PD&F goals also should repeatedly help each student understand how the student is building on earlier knowledge, skills, and capacities. A student's growth on the four goals occurs in the context of the student's preexisting stage of development on ownership over the student's own continuous development (self-directed learning), responsibility and service orientation to others, and creative problem solving and good judgment. For example, many law students have substantial earlier experience with teamwork/collaboration or work requiring a service orientation. The curriculum – including mentoring and coaching – should focus on the intersection between the learner's preexisting stage of development on these outcomes and the developmental stages the student must demonstrate to grow toward the level of competence of a practicing lawyer.

4.8 PRINCIPLE 8 THINK VERY DIFFERENTLY ABOUT ASSESSMENT ON PD&F GOALS

Combine guided self-assessment with direct observation and multi-source feedback and assessment by faculty and staff.

Assessment to foster each student's growth toward later stages of development on each of the four PD&F goals is going to be different from the

---

[96] Gantt & Madison, *supra* note 8, at 503–04.
[97] JEFFREY ARNETT, EMERGING ADULTHOOD 313 (2d ed. 2015).
[98] *Id.*

straightforward reliance on written examinations or papers common in law school classes. Those methods have some place, but they are not geared principally to the task at hand. ABA accreditation standard 314 requires a law school to use both formative[99] and summative[100] assessment methods in its program of legal education to measure and improve student learning and provide meaningful feedback to students.[101] With those accreditation requirements in mind, we outline here practicable strategies for assessments on PD&F goals.

Lessons from competency-based medical education (CBME) are especially instructive here. The reader is advised to remember, however, that medical education has been in the business of purposeful support of professional identity formation for many years. Legal education is just embarking on its journey. We look here at assessment in medical education for illumination and its power of suggestion. It invites one to see how the assessment might be structured and conducted as legal education evolves in its support of PD&F goals.

In Chapter 3, we presented Table 12 that compared CBME to the traditional time-based (number of exposure hours) medical education that resembles traditional legal education. As Table 12 notes, assessment in a well-conceived competency-based educational model should include not just written exams and papers but also multiple assessment measures employing assessment tools that are "authentic" in the sense that they are or mimic actual professional work. Both formative and summative assessment will be needed. And the parties participating in the assessment process will be more numerous and varied. As explored in Chapter 2, both faculty and staff – in a "whole building" approach – are important observers of each student's development with respect to the four PD&F goals. They thus can contribute to the assessment process.

To draw assessment of PD&F goals into clearer view, a key initial step is to look at the modules currently in the curriculum that foster student growth regarding any of the goals. Our Principle 1, you will recall, encourages the

---

99   *Standard 314. Assessment of Student Learning, Interpretation 314–1, 2021-2022 Standards and Rules of Procedure for Approval of Law Schools*, A.B.A. SECTION OF LEGAL EDUC. & ADMISSIONS TO THE BAR [hereinafter *ABA Standards*]. Formative assessment methods are measurements at different points during a particular course or at different points over the span of a student's education that provide meaningful feedback to improve student learning.

100 *Id.* Summative assessment methods are measurements at the culmination of a particular course or at the culmination of any part of a student's legal education that measure the degree of student learning.

101 *Standard 314. Assessment of Student Learning, ABA Standards, supra* note 99.

faculty and staff to envision progress along any PD&F goal as a process of stage development marked by the attainment of measurable Milestones. Principle 2 encourages faculty and staff to strive for curriculum and assessment modules that are coordinated and build on each other progressively. How does the current curriculum look? Does it present a linear progression of curriculum and assessment modules to foster student growth toward later stages of development of the particular goal? Are there gaps?

Another key initial step is to next ask in which modules faculty and staff will be able to actually observe each student and make informed judgments about the student's stage of development on a particular goal. With that step done, you have identified significant opportunities for assessment.

Note that the assessment contemplated here is *direct observation of students in authentic (real-life or mimicking real-life) professional experiences.* In CBME, this kind of direct observation is mandatory for the reliable and valid assessment of PD&F competencies,[102] and we see no reason for disregarding that principle when considering PD&F goals in legal education. The direct observation contemplated here is considered a form of workplace-based assessment, with a student's day-to-day work in an authentic professional experience observed and assessed. It is an assessment strategy that looks not only for what a student knows cognitively but also for whether a student "shows how" in a simulation or what a student "does" in a practice setting.[103]

Multi-source feedback, widely used in CBME and also referred to as a "360-degree" assessment,[104] "is an assessment that is completed by multiple persons within a learner's sphere of influence. Multi-rater assessments in CBME are ideally completed by other students, peers, nurses, faculty supervisors, patients, families and the residents themselves."[105] Different respondents focus on the characteristics of the student or physician that they can assess; patients, for example, are not expected to assess clinical expertise.[106]

---

[102] *See* Jennifer Kogan & Eric Holmboe, *Direct Observation, in* ERIC HOLMBOE ET AL., EVALUATION OF CLINICAL COMPETENCE 61 (2d ed. 2018).

[103] *See* G. E. Miller, *The Assessment of Clinical Skills/Competence/Performance*, 65 ACAD. MED. 63–67 (No. 9, 1990).

[104] Ahmed Al Ansari et al., *The Construct and Criterion Validity of the Multi-Source Feedback Process to Assess Physician Performance: A Meta-Analysis*, 5 ADVANCES IN MED. EDUC. & PRAC. 39 (2014).

[105] Linda Snell, *Supporting Professionalism and Professional Identity Formation at the Postgraduate Level, in* TEACHING MEDICAL PROFESSIONALISM, *supra* note 79, at 248, 254 (2016).

[106] Tyrone Donnon et al., *The Reliability, Validity, and Feasibility of Multisource Feedback Physician Assessment: A Systematic Review*, 89 ACAD. MED. 1 (2014).

High-quality assessment will use rating scales, evaluation forms, and the aggregation of multiple data points.[107] To provide reliability and validity, multiple assessors using multiple methods are required. Good observational assessment requires broad sampling across different encounters.[108] Together with rating scales and evaluation forms, narrative feedback also is very useful as feedback to the student.[109]

A meta-analysis of the multi-source feedback process to assess physician performance[110] emphasizes that multi-source feedback "has been shown to be a unique form of evaluation that provides more valuable information than any single feedback source. [Multi-source feedback] has gained widespread acceptance both for formative and summative assessment of professionals, and is seen as a trigger for reflecting on where changes in practice are required."[111] In addition, "[Multi-source feedback] has been shown to enhance changes in clinical performance, communication skills, professionalism, teamwork, productivity, and building trusting relationships with patients."[112] A second meta-analysis of multi-source feedback also concludes that it is reliable, valid, and feasible.[113]

CBME assessment of observable behaviors also includes recording all instances of unprofessional conduct, for example, when a learner does not meet the requirements of the student conduct code or the profession's code.[114] All University of Texas system medical schools, for instance, have developed some mechanism for identifying and recording student lapses in professionalism and engaging the student to reflect on the lapses.[115]

How might the foregoing CBME assessment approach translate to legal education? Each law student might be required, for instance, to complete a regular self-assessment using a Milestone Model of the student's stage of

---

[107]   John J. Norcini & Judy A. Shea, *Assessment of Professionalism and Progress in the Development of a Professional Identity, in* TEACHING MEDICAL PROFESSIONALISM, *supra* note 79, at 155, 162.

[108]   *Id.* at 162–63.

[109]   Al Ansari et al., *supra* note 104, at 42.

[110]   The meta-analysis included 35 studies. The sample size of the studies ranges from 6 plastic surgery residents to 577 pediatric residents who had been assessed using multi-source feedback with as few as 1.2 patients and 2.6 medical colleagues to as many as 47.3 patients completing forms per student. *Id.*

[111]   *Id.* at 39.

[112]   *Id.* at 49.

[113]   Donnon et al., *supra* note 106, at 5.

[114]   Norcini & Shea, *supra* note 108 at 162.

[115]   Mark Holden et al., *Developing and Implementing an Undergraduate Curriculum, in* TEACHING MEDICAL PROFESSIONALISM, *supra* note 79 at 231, 239–40.

development on one or more of the four PD&F goals – especially after a significant authentic professional experience (in keeping with Principle 6). The student could be required to have good supporting evidence before selecting a stage of development. The burden might be placed on each student to seek out assessments, especially by direct observation by faculty and staff. Faculty and staff could use a relevant Milestone Model to assess the student's stage of development. The law school's curriculum and culture would encourage each student actively to seek experiences and assessments and feedback – and to reflect on the feedback to determine how to grow to the next level of development. Table 18 indicates opportunities for direct observations of students on the four PD&F goals that exist in the typical law school.

A long-term mentor/coach relationship is going to provide strong longitudinal observations and feedback. As discussed earlier in Principle 5, if each student meets regularly with a mentor/coach, the mentor/coach can facilitate guided reflection and guided self-assessment, including comparing the student's self-assessment with the observations and assessments of faculty and staff. The coach then helps the student decide on the next action steps to grow to the next level on a competency. The coach can also provide an assessment using the relevant Milestone Model.

TABLE 18 *Law school faculty and staff observing students on any of the four PD&F goals (especially in authentic professional experiences)*

All full-time and adjunct faculty supervising student projects that mimic real-life lawyer work like memos, presentations, briefs, and drafting legal documents, and including research assistant work

Experiential faculty like those teaching a clinic, lawyering skills, externships, simulations like negotiation, ADR, or trial advocacy

All staff assisting in the clinics or experiences

Supervisors of competitions like Moot Court, Negotiation, or ADR

Clients (in clinical settings)

Career services staff

Academic support and student services staff

Librarians working with students on projects

Student peers in work for credit or in student organizations on a competency like teamwork/collaboration

Mentor/coaches

4.9 PRINCIPLE 9 STUDENT PORTFOLIOS CAN HELP STUDENTS PROGRESS

Consider calling upon each student to create a personal portfolio on any one of the four PD&F goals, including an individualized learning plan to develop to the next level of growth.[116]

Comparing traditional time-based (number of exposure hours) legal education with competency-based legal education, Table 12 in Chapter 3 makes clear that the "driving force for the process" in competency-based education for each student's growth toward later stages of a goal shifts from the teacher to the student. Portfolios created and managed by the student help execute the shift. The student carries the burden to gather and demonstrate credible evidence that the student is growing to the next level on a competency. Portfolios are a very promising tool for empowering a student to be the driving force in the student's development.

A portfolio is a "purposeful collection of student work that demonstrates the student's efforts and progress in selected domains."[117] In addition, "[p]ortfolios are recommended for capturing the combined assessments [for a student] and providing a longitudinal perspective."[118] Drs. Holden, Buck, and Luk note that "[t]he aggregation of information into a portfolio would provide longitudinal perspective allowing for a broader view of students' developmental trajectory not readily available from more narrow or discrete pieces of information."[119] An E-Portfolio is simply a digital repository for the purposeful collection of the student's work in one place. It enables each student, working with faculty and staff, to "create evidence of learning in creative ways that are not possible with typical paper-based methods. For example, E-Portfolios enable learners to demonstrate, reflect upon, and easily share scholarly and other work products using graphics, video, web links, and presentations."[120]

---

[116]   Some of the material in this section is taken from Neil Hamilton, *Formation-of-an-Ethical-Professional Identity (Professionalism) Learning Outcomes and E-Portfolio Formative Assessments*, 48 U. Pac. L. Rev. 847–73 (2017).

[117]   Yvonne Steinert, *Educational Theory and Strategies to Support Professionalism and Professional Identity Formation*, in Teaching Medical Professionalism, *supra* note 79, at 68, 78 (quoting Adrina L. Kalet et al., *Promoting Professional Development Portfolio: Successes, Joys, and Frustrations*, 82 Acad. Med. 1068 (2007)).

[118]   Holden et al., *supra* note 115, at 236.

[119]   *Id.* at 237.

[120]   Laurie Posey et al., *Developing a Pathway for an Institution Wide ePortfolio Program*, 5 Int'l J. E-Portfolio 75, 75 (2015).

A medical education survey indicates the potential benefits of portfolios. By 2016, more than 45 percent of the medical schools in the United States were using student portfolios, with 72 percent of those using a longitudinal, competency-based portfolio strategy.[121] Eighty percent of students and 69 percent of faculty agreed that portfolios engage students. Ninety-seven percent of the faculty respondents agreed that there is room for improvement with respect to the use of portfolios.[122] A systemic review of all the empirical evidence on the education effects of using portfolios found that "the 'higher quality' studies identified by the authors suggest benefits to student reflection and self-awareness knowledge and understanding (including the integration of theory and practice) and preparedness for postgraduate training in which the keeping of a portfolio and engagement in reflective practice are increasingly important."[123] To avoid student, faculty, and staff burnout, it is important to limit portfolios to no more than a few competencies that are the most important for the school.[124]

An E-Portfolio curricular strategy applied by a law school to the student's stages of development for teamwork or team leadership, for example, would require each student to collect evidence that demonstrates later-stage development of this competency. The student then selects the most credible and persuasive evidence that the student has achieved a particular stage of development. The student carries the burden to demonstrate that they are at a competent learner stage on teamwork or team leadership. The student therefore would need to contemplate what is the most persuasive evidence for audiences such as law faculty and staff, as well as audiences such as legal employers in the student's areas of employment interest. The student then reflects on what the student needs to do to grow to the next stage of development regarding that competency and how to develop credible evidence of that growth. The student creates an individualized learning plan containing action items to grow to the next level, including authentic professional experiences and identification of the needed direct observations by faculty and staff.

Portfolios offer additional benefits than can merit noting. A portfolio approach to assessment

---

[121] Jason Chertoff et al., *Status of Portfolios in Undergraduate Medical Education in the LCME Accredited US Medical School*, 38 MED. TEACH. 886, 889 (2016).

[122] *Id.*

[123] Sharon Buckley et al., *The Educational Effects of Portfolios on Undergraduate Student Learning: A Best Evidence Medical Education (BEME) Systematic Review*, 31 MED. TEACH. 282, 293 (2009).

[124] J. Donald Boudreau, *The Evolution of an Undergraduate Medical Program on Professionalism and Identity Formation, in* TEACHING MEDICAL PROFESSIONALISM, *supra* note 79, at 217, 226 (2016).

1. Provides a central location where all the observations from different stakeholders about a student's performance regarding a competency are collected;
2. produces a collection of the student's own on-going reflection into a longitudinal file;
3. assists mentoring and coaching, as the mentor/coach reviews a student's portfolio on a given competency to provide feedback (and these mentor/coach observations, in turn, should be included in the portfolio); and
4. regularizes the student's development of a written individualized learning plan that is revised regularly based on new experiences, feedback, and further reflection. The student is collecting the most persuasive evidence of later stage development on particular competencies.

4.10 PRINCIPLE 10 PROGRAM ASSESSMENT ON PD&F GOALS BECOMES CLEAR AND MANAGEABLE IF PRINCIPLES 1 THROUGH 9 ARE HEEDED AND IMPLEMENTED

Progress on Principles 1 through 9, and particularly on Principles 1, 2, 4, 5, 8, and 9, will substantially support program assessment as required by ABA Accreditation Standard 315.

In time – exactly when will depend on how quickly law school and university accreditors move – a law school will be required to undertake program assessment on each institutional learning outcome that includes a PD&F goal to satisfy accreditation requirements.[125] A law school that puts Principles 1 through 9 into effective action – and particularly Principles 1, 2, 4, 5, 8, and 9 – will be creating a foundation for effective program assessment on any of the PD&F goals.

ABA Standard 315 currently requires "ongoing evaluation of the law school's program of legal education, learning outcomes, and assessment methods" and provides that the faculty "shall use the results of this evaluation to determine degree of student attainment of competency in the learning outcomes and to make appropriate changes to improve the curriculum."[126] ABA Interpretation 315–1 provides a number of examples of program evaluation methods

---

[125] *See Standard 315. Evaluation of Program of Legal Education Learning Outcomes, and Assessment Methods, ABA Standards, supra note 99.*
[126] *Id.*

including: review of the records the law school maintains to measure individual student achievement pursuant to Standard 314;[127] evaluation of student learning portfolios; student evaluation of the sufficiency of their education; student performance in capstone courses or other courses that appropriately assess a variety of skills and knowledge; bar exam passage rates; placement rates; surveys of attorneys, judges, and alumni; and assessment of student performance by judges, attorneys, or law professors from other schools.[128]

For law schools that are within a university, the accreditation standards that the university must meet will differentiate between direct and indirect assessments and will require some direct assessment (also called direct measures) of student performance of a learning outcome competency. For example, the Council for Higher Education Accreditation now requires direct measures of student learning:

> Evidence of student learning outcomes can take many forms, but should involve direct examination of student performance – either for individual students or a representative sample of students. Examples of the types of direct-measure evidence that might be used appropriately in accreditation settings include (but are not limited to):
>
> - faculty-designed comprehensive capstone examinations and assignments;
> - performance on licensing or other external examinations;
> - professionally judged performances or demonstrations of abilities in context;
> - portfolios of student work compiled over time; and
> - samples of representative student work generated in response to typical course assignments.[129]

---

[127] ABA accreditation standard 314 requires a law school to use both formative and summative assessment methods in its program of legal education to measure and improve student learning and provide meaningful feedback to students. *Standard 314. Assessment of Student Learning*, ABA Standards, *supra* note 99.

[128] *See Standard 315, Interpretation 315-1*, ABA Standards, *supra* note 99.

[129] Council for Higher Education Accreditation, *Statement of Mutual Responsibilities for Student Learning Outcomes: Accreditation, Institutions, and Programs* 5 (2003). To give another example, the Higher Learning Commission, one of six regional institutional accreditors in the United States, accredits degree-granting post-secondary educational institutions in the North Central region, which includes nineteen states. The Higher Learning Commission requires universities (including the law schools within a university) to demonstrate "documents and reports using direct measures for the assessment of student learning." Higher Learning Commission, *Providing Evidence for the Criteria for Accreditation*, https://download .hlcommission.org/ProvidingEvidence2020_INF.pdf

A key point about program assessment for a law school to understand going forward is that the current ABA Standard 315 on program assessment is probably less demanding than the accreditation standards of the university of which the law school is a part. While ABA Standard 315 includes student evaluation of the sufficiency of their education (an indirect measure), the university standards will require at least one if not two direct measures on a PD&F goal in a law school's institutional learning outcomes. It would be efficient to plan ultimately to meet the university's standards.

A law school considering program assessment on any of the PD&F goals will benefit greatly from having a Milestone Model on the PD&F goal the school has incorporated in its learning outcomes, as contemplated by Principle 1. The law school can define the level of development that the school expects a target percentage of its students to achieve by graduation. Then the school can define the most practicable, least costly, and most efficient direct measure to assess whether the target percentage of students achieved that level of development. Implementation of Principle 2, which suggests a sequenced progression of modules in the curriculum for a PD&F goal, will provide a curriculum map of where best to assess student. Following Principles 4 and 5 will have each student writing guided reflections observed by a mentor/coach that can serve as direct measures of development on a PD&F goal. Principle 8 (on thinking differently about assessment) emphasizes the importance of direct observations of students performing a PD&F competency by faculty and staff including adjuncts, mentors, and coaches who observe student performance. These observers can assess each student's stage of development using a Milestone Model. Principle 9 suggests consideration of portfolios, with the burden placed on each student to gather evidence demonstrating that the student has achieved the required level of development on a Milestone Model.

The development of practicable and efficient direct measures is an excellent area for cooperation among groups of law schools that have adopted any of the same PD&F goals.

APPENDIX B

Milestone Models for All Four PD&F Goals

What would a Milestone Model for each of the four PD&F goals look like? Milestones for each are analyzed here. A Holloran Center working group created the Milestone Model for goal 1, and the authors created the Milestone Models for goals 2–4.

1 MILESTONE MODEL FOR GOAL 1 – OWNERSHIP OF CONTINUOUS PROFESSIONAL DEVELOPMENT TOWARD EXCELLENCE AT THE MAJOR COMPETENCIES THAT CLIENTS, EMPLOYERS, AND THE LEGAL SYSTEM NEED

Since 2017, the Holloran Center has organized working groups to create Milestone Models on the most common learning outcomes the law schools are adopting that relate to the four PD&F goals. The consensus of these expert panels creates some content validity for the models. As of June 2020, 33 percent of the 186 law schools that posted their learning outcomes had adopted a learning outcome related to self-directedness, self-regulatedness, or ownership over the student's own development learning outcome.[1] Table 19 is the current Holloran Center Milestone Model on ownership over the student's own development/self-directed learning. Note that this Milestone Model matches up both with Goal 1 – ownership of continuous professional development toward excellence at the major competencies that clients, employers, and the legal system need – and with the right side of the Foundational Competencies Model discussed in Figure 1 in Chapter 1 (the competencies that clients and employers want).[2]

The Holloran Center is developing Milestone Models on other competencies related to a student's ownership of their continuous professional

---

[1] These data are available on the Holloran Center website. https://www.stthomas.edu/holloran left/learningoutcomesandprofessionaldevelopment/learningoutcomesdatabase/

[2] The Holloran Center Working Group on Self-Directed Learning created this model. The members are Kendell Kerew (chair), Rupa Bandari, Susan Fine, Neil Hamilton, and Benjamin Madison. This model is a synthesis of the data available from large-firm competency models and the American Association of Colleges and Universities rubric on life-long learning. For the law firm models, *see* NEIL W. HAMILTON, ROADMAP: THE LAW STUDENT'S GUIDE TO MEANINGFUL EMPLOYMENT 63–69 (2d. ed. 2018) (hereinafter ROADMAP). For the AAC&U model, see American Association of Colleges and Universities, *Foundations and Skills for Lifelong Learning VALUE Rubric* (2009), www.aacu.org/value/rubrics/lifelong-learning.

TABLE 19 *Holloran Center Milestone Model on assessment of student's ownership of continuous professional development (self-directedness)*

Sub-competencies of Ownership/Self-Directedness	Novice Learner (Level 1)	Intermediate Learner (Level 2)	Competent Learner (Level 3)	Exceptional Learner (Level 4)
1. Self-Assesses and Identifies Strengths and Areas for Growth *Understands full range of lawyering competencies and diagnoses learning needs*	RARELY demonstrates understanding of full range of lawyering competencies and diagnoses learning needs	SOMETIMES demonstrates understanding of full range of lawyering competencies and diagnoses learning needs	OFTEN demonstrates understanding of full range of lawyering competencies and diagnoses learning needs	CONSISTENTLY demonstrates understanding of full range of lawyering competencies and diagnoses learning needs
2. Articulates Goals and Follows a Plan *Implements a written professional development plan reflecting goals that are specific, measurable, achievable, relevant, and time bound[3]*	RARELY creates and implements a written professional development plan reflecting goals that are specific, measurable, achievable, relevant and time-bound	SOMETIMES creates and implements a written professional development plan reflecting goals that are specific, measurable, achievable, relevant and time-bound	OFTEN creates and implements a written professional development plan reflecting goals that are specific, measurable, achievable, relevant and time-bound	CONSISTENTLY creates and implements a written professional development plan reflecting goals that are specific, measurable, achievable, relevant and time-bound
3. Acquires and Learns from Experience *Seeks experiences to develop competencies and meet articulated goals and seeks and incorporates feedback received during the experiences*	RARELY seeks experiences or seeks and incorporates feedback received during the experiences	SOMETIMES seeks experiences and seeks and incorporates feedback received during the experiences	OFTEN seeks experiences and seeks and incorporates feedback received during the experiences	CONSISTENTLY seeks experiences and seeks and incorporates feedback received during the experiences

3   Goals that exhibit these factors are referred to as SMART Goals: Specific – clear goals including what, why, and how; Measurable – including a clear method for evaluation of progress; Achievable – including obstacles and realistic solutions; Relevant – including connection to core values; and Time-bound – including a clear timeline of steps.

4. Reflects and Applies Lessons Learned	RARELY	SOMETIMES	OFTEN	CONSISTENTLY
Uses *reflective practice*[4] to reflect on performance, contemplate lessons learned, identify how to apply lessons learned to improve in the future, and applies those lessons	uses reflective practice to reflect on performance, contemplate lessons learned, identify how to apply lessons learned to improve in the future, and applies those lessons	uses reflective practice to reflect on performance, contemplate lessons learned, identify how to apply lessons learned to improve in the future, and applies those lessons	uses reflective practice to reflect on performance, contemplate lessons learned, identify how to apply lessons learned to improve in the future, and applies those lessons	uses reflective practice to reflect on performance, contemplate lessons learned, identify how to apply lessons learned to improve in the future, and applies those lessons

4 *See* the discussion of reflection at Principle 5 of this Chapter 4, *supra.*

development including (1) grit and resilience, (2) growth mindset, and (3) self-awareness. These will be available on the center's website in spring 2022.[5]

2 MILESTONE MODEL FOR GOAL 2 – A DEEP RESPONSIBILITY AND SERVICE ORIENTATION TO OTHERS, ESPECIALLY THE CLIENT

A Milestone Model for Goal 2 – a deep responsibility and service orientation to others, especially the client – is trying to capture the stages of development of a fiduciary disposition or fiduciary mindset, using "fiduciary" in the general meaning of being founded on trustworthiness.[6] Deep care for the client is the principal foundation for client trust in the individual lawyer and the profession itself.[7] Each law student and new lawyer must learn to internalize a responsibility to put both the client's and the legal system's interests before the lawyer's self-interest (minimally as required by the law of lawyering and aspirationally as reflected in the core values and ideals of the profession).

Unlike with Goal 1, law schools have not generally been adopting learning outcomes with language that specifically emphasizes deep responsibility and service orientation to others, especially the client. However, significant numbers of law schools have been adopting learning outcomes that, at their foundation, rest upon a deep responsibility and service orientation to others. For example, of the 186 law schools that had posted learning outcomes by June 2020:

Thirty-eight percent include a learning outcome on understanding the value of providing pro bono service to the disadvantaged;

Thirty-three percent include a learning outcome on teamwork/collaboration;

Twenty-seven percent include a cross-cultural competency learning outcome;

Twenty-seven percent include a version of a professionalism or high ethical standards learning outcome (which related to trustworthiness in relationships);

Fifteen percent include a learning outcome on integrity (which also relates to trustworthiness in relationships);

---

[5] https://www.stthomas.edu/hollorancenter/hollorancompetencymilestones/

[6] *See* William M. Sullivan, *Foreword* to TEACHING MEDICAL PROFESSIONALISM: SUPPORTING THE DEVELOPMENT OF A PROFESSIONAL IDENTITY ix (Richard L. Cruess et al. eds., 2d ed. 2016) [hereinafter TEACHING MEDICAL PROFESSIONALISM]; William Sullivan, *Align Preparation with Practice*, 85 N.Y. ST. B.A. J. (No. 7 Sept. 2013) at 41–43 (where he introduces the concept of fiduciary disposition). See also *supra* page 6 (discussing fiduciary mindset).

[7] Sullivan, *Foreword* to TEACHING MEDICAL PROFESSIONALISM, *supra* note 6, at xi, xv.

> Thirteen percent include a learning outcome on interviewing, counseling, or both;
> Twelve percent include a learning outcome on active listening;
> Six percent include a learning outcome on respect for others;
> Six percent include a learning outcome on leadership; and
> Five percent include a learning outcome on client-centered problem solving.

The Holloran Center has Milestone Models posted on teamwork/collaboration, team leadership, cultural competency, honoring commitments, and integrity[8] and has working groups developing Milestone Models on pro bono activity, active listening, leadership, and professional communication. There is not yet a working group creating a Milestone Model specifically on Goal 2, but the model will look like that in Table 20.

The sub-competencies of Table 20's Milestone Model on Goal 2 are at an abstract level and thus challenging for faculty and staff to observe and assess. Practically speaking, faculty and staff could observe and assess competencies like commitment to pro bono service, cultural competency, teamwork/collaboration, team leadership, and active listening, which reflect a student's responsibility and service to others and are in language that clients and employers understand and value.

3 MILESTONE MODEL FOR GOAL 3 – A CLIENT-CENTERED PROBLEM-SOLVING APPROACH AND GOOD JUDGMENT THAT GROUND EACH STUDENT'S RESPONSIBILITY AND SERVICE TO THE CLIENT

A Milestone Model for Goal 3 – a client-centered problem-solving approach and good judgment that ground each student's responsibility and service to the client – goes beyond ABA Standard 302's minimum requirement that each law school shall establish learning outcomes that include the competency of "legal analysis and reasoning" and "problem-solving."[9]

Many legal educators define legal analysis and reasoning and problem solving to include some version of the IRAC formulation familiar to law students – Issue correctly identified from facts, Rule correctly identified and explained, Application providing a well-reasoned discussion relating the facts

---

[8] https://www.stthomas.edu/hollorancenter/hollorancompetencymilestones/
[9] *Standard 302. Learning Outcomes, 2021-2022 Standards and Rules of Procedure for Approval of Law Schools*, A.B.A. SECTION OF LEGAL EDUC. & ADMISSIONS TO THE BAR.

TABLE 20 *Milestone Model on assessment of student's stage of development on a deep responsibility and service orientation to others, especially the client*

Sub-competencies of Internalized Deep Responsibility and Service to Others	Novice Learner (Level 1)	Intermediate Learner (Level 2)	Competent Learner (Level 3)	Exceptional Learner (Level 4)
1. Reflects on and can explain own principles/core values on responsibilities and service to others	RARELY reflects on own principles and values on responsibilities and service to others	SOMETIMES reflects on own principles and values on responsibilities and service to others	OFTEN reflects on own principles and values on responsibilities and service to others	CONSISTENTLY reflects on own principles and values on responsibilities and service to others
2. Seeks experiences involving responsibilities to others on matters important to them and reflects on experiences	RARELY seeks experiences involving responsibilities to others on matters important to them and reflects on experiences	SOMETIMES seeks experiences involving responsibilities to others on matters important to them and reflects on experiences	OFTEN seeks experiences involving responsibilities to others on matters important to them and reflects on experiences	CONSISTENTLY seeks experiences involving responsibilities to others on matters important to them and reflects on experiences
3. Seeks understanding of law of lawyering regarding responsibilities and service to client and others	RARELY seeks understanding of law of lawyering regarding responsibilities and service to client and others	SOMETIMES seeks understanding of law of lawyering regarding responsibilities and service to client and others	OFTEN seeks understanding of law of lawyering regarding responsibilities and service to client and others	CONSISTENTLY seeks understanding of law of lawyering regarding responsibilities and service to client and others

	RARELY	SOMETIMES	OFTEN	CONSISTENTLY
4. Recognizes law of lawyering issues in the most common experiential situations involving responsibilities to clients or others and is able to analyze and manage such issues	recognizes law of lawyering issues in the most common experiential situations involving responsibilities to clients or others and is able to analyze and manage such issues	recognizes law of lawyering issues in the most common experiential situations involving responsibilities to clients or others and is able to analyze and manage such issues	recognizes law of lawyering issues in the most common experiential situations involving responsibilities to clients or others and is able to analyze and manage such issues	recognizes law of lawyering issues in the most common experiential situations involving responsibilities to clients or others and is able to analyze and manage such issues
5. Seeks understanding of profession's ideals and core values regarding responsibilities to client and others	seeks understanding of profession's ideals and core values regarding responsibilities to client and others	seeks understanding of profession's ideals and core values regarding responsibilities to client and others	seeks understanding of profession's ideals and core values regarding responsibilities to client and others	seeks understanding of profession's ideals and core values regarding responsibilities to client and others
6. Seeks experience and reflects on experience to integrate law of lawyering and profession's ideals and core values regarding responsibilities to client and others into own first principles/core values	seeks experience and reflects on experience to integrate law of lawyering and profession's ideals and core values regarding responsibilities to client and others into own first principles/core values	seeks experience and reflects on experience to integrate law of lawyering and profession's ideals and core values regarding responsibilities to client and others into own first principles/core values	seeks experience and reflects on experience to integrate law of lawyering and profession's ideals and core values regarding responsibilities to client and others into own first principles/core values	seeks experience and reflects on experience to integrate law of lawyering and profession's ideals and core values regarding responsibilities to client and others into own first principles/core values

to the rules, and Conclusion explained logically convincingly.[10] A later-stage IRAC skill is foundational for legal analysis and reasoning and problem-solving, but Goal 3's "client-centered problem-solving and good judgment" involve additional skills beyond IRAC. Those competencies include deeply understanding the client's context (and where applicable, business), values, and preferences. Client-centered problem solving and good judgment also involve career-long habits of (1) trying to understand legal issues in broader contexts and (2) seeking challenging professional experiences and reflecting on them to continually improve.[11] As is illustrated in Figure 2 in Chapter 2, client-centered problem solving is a compound competency in Group 4. It builds on two foundational PD&F goals (Group 1), technical legal skills (Group 2), and basic individual and relational building block competencies (Group 3).

Client-centered problem solving and good judgment can borrow from the concept of coproduction in the delivery of health services. Coproduction of a service in a physician/patient (or lawyer/client) relationship is based on (1) the service provider's deep understanding of the patient's (or client's) context, (2) effective communication, (3) deeper understanding of one another's expertise and values, (4) more cultivation of shared goals, and (5) more mutuality in responsibility and accountability for performance.[12]

Table 21 provides a Milestone Model on client-centered problem solving and good judgment that is adapted from the American Association of Colleges and Universities Problem-Solving Value Rubric.[13] Building on a version of legal analysis and reasoning like IRAC, client-centered problem solving and good judgment involve a process of partnering with the client to define the

---

[10]   See Kelley Burton, *Using a Legal Reasoning Grid and Criterion-Referenced Assessment Rubic on IRAC (Issue, Rule, Application, and Conclusion)*, 10 J. Learning Design (No. 2 2017) (providing a stage development model on IRAC), www.jld.edu.au/article/view/229/283.html

[11]   See Patrick E. Longan, Daisy H. Floyd & Timothy W. Floyd, The Formation of Professional Identity: The Path from Student to Lawyer 106–11 (2020).

[12]   Maren Batalden et al, *Coproduction of Health Care*, 25 BMJ Qual. S. F. 509, 511 (2016). ROADMAP, *supra* note 2, at 8. Jordan Furlong writes, "[l]aw firms should think of their clients ... as 'co-producers' ... answering some their own questions and solving some of their own problems, but doing so alongside their other providers, in tandem and ideally in collaboration." Jordan Furlong, Law Is a Buyer's Market: Building a Client-First Law Firm 129–30 (2017). Law firms and clients, as co-providers, are partners and colleagues in the quest to achieve the client's objectives. *Id.*

[13]   See American Association of Colleges and Universities, *Problem-Solving VALUE Rubric*, https://www.aacu.org/value/rubrics/problem-solving.
       The VALUE rubrics were developed by teams of faculty experts representing colleges and universities across the United States through a process that examined many existing campus rubrics and related documents for each learning outcome and incorporated additional feedback from faculty. The rubrics articulate fundamental criteria for each learning outcome, with performance descriptors demonstrating progressively more sophisticated levels of attainment.

TABLE 21 *Milestone Model on client-centered problem solving and good judgment*

Sub-competencies of Client-Centered Problem Solving/Good Judgment	Novice Learner (Level 1)	Intermediate Learner (Level 2)	Competent Learner (Level 3)	Exceptional Learner (Level 4)
1. Seeks Deep Understanding of Client's Context (Business), Values, and Preferences	RARELY seeks deep understanding of client's context (business), values and preferences	SOMETIMES seeks deep understanding of client's context (business), values, and preferences	OFTEN seeks deep understanding of client's context business), values, and preferences	CONSISTENTLY seeks deep understanding of client's context (business), values, and preferences
2. Partnering with the Client, Defines Problem	RARELY demonstrates active listening with client	SOMETIMES demonstrates active listening with client	OFTEN demonstrates active listening with client	CONSISTENTLY demonstrates active listening with client
	RARELY demonstrates an ability to partner with the client to construct a complete problem statement with the relevant contextual factors	SOMETIMES demonstrates the ability to partner with the client to construct a complete problem statement with relevant contextual factors	OFTEN demonstrates the ability to partner with the client to construct a complete problem statement with relevant contextual factors	CONSISTENTLY demonstrates the ability to partner with the client to construct a complete problem statement with all relevant contextual factors
3. Partnering with the Client, Identifies Strategies and Proposes Solutions	RARELY identifies a strategy and proposes a clear solution for solving the problem	SOMETIMES identifies a strategy and proposes a solution that is "off the shelf" rather than individually designed to address the specific contextual factors of the problem	OFTEN identifies multiple strategies and proposes one or more solutions that indicate comprehension of the problem; solutions are sensitive to contextual factors	CONSISTENTLY identifies multiple strategies and proposes one or more solutions/hypotheses that indicate a deep comprehension of the problem; solutions are sensitive to contextual factors

TABLE 21 (continued)

Sub-competencies of Client-Centered Problem Solving/Good Judgment	Novice Learner (Level 1)	Intermediate Learner (Level 2)	Competent Learner (Level 3)	Exceptional Learner (Level 4)
4. Partnering with the Client, Helps Client Evaluate Potential Solutions	RARELY goes beyond superficial evaluation of solutions (for example, contains cursory, surface-level explanation) in terms of the history of the problem, logic/reasoning, feasibility of solution, and impacts of solution	SOMETIMES goes beyond superficial evaluation of solutions but evaluation is brief (for example, explanation lacks depth) in terms of the history of the problem, logic/reasoning, feasibility of solution, and impacts of solution	OFTEN evaluation of solutions is adequate (for example, contains thorough explanation) in terms of the history of the problem, logic/reasoning, feasibility of solution, and impacts of solution	CONSISTENTLY evaluation of solutions is deep and elegant (for example, contains thorough and insightful explanation) and is deep and thorough in terms of the history of problem, logic/reasoning, feasibility of solution, and impacts of solution
5. Assists Client in Implementing Solution	RARELY implements the client's solution in a manner that directly addresses the problem statement	SOMETIMES implements the client's solution in a manner that directly addresses the problem statement	OFTEN implements the client's solution in a manner that directly addresses the problem statement	CONSISTENTLY implements the client's solution in a manner that directly addresses the problem statement

problem, identify strategies, propose solutions, evaluate the potential solutions, and assist in implementing the solutions.

4 MILESTONE MODEL FOR GOAL 4 – WELL-BEING PRACTICES

A Milestone Model for Goal 4 – well-being practices – can build on Self-Determination Theory's (SDT) three basic psychological needs and the four intrinsic values that Krieger and Sheldon have identified as contributing to student and lawyer well-being discussed in Chapter 1. The three basic psychological SDT needs are (1) autonomy (to feel in control of the person's own goals and behaviors), (2) competence (to feel the person has the needed skills to be successful), and (3) relatedness (to experience a sense of belonging or attachment to other people). SDT also identifies four intrinsic values that mirror the three basic psychological needs and lead to behaviors that fulfill the three basic needs and thus promote well-being. The four intrinsic values are (1) self-understanding/growth (the importance of learning and personal growth), (2) intimacy with others (the importance of trusting close relationship with others), (3) helping others (improving others' lives, especially those in need), and (4) being in and building community (improving society).

Note that Figure 2 in Chapter 2 identifies well-being practices as a competency in Group 3 – Basic Individual and Relational Building Block Competencies – that is building on the two foundational learning outcomes discussed earlier: Goal 1 is internalizing ownership of continuous professional development toward excellence and Goal 2 is internalizing deep responsibilities and service to others, especially the client. SDT's psychological need for "competence" and the intrinsic value of learning and personal growth is realized if a student grows to later stages of Goal 1. SDT's psychological need for "relatedness" and the three intrinsic values of (1) trusting close relationships, (2) helping others, and (3) being in and building community are animated by a person's growth toward later stages of Goal 2, internalizing deep responsibilities and service to others, especially the client, and Goal 3, client-centered problem solving.

Table 22 provides a Milestone Model for well-being practices.[14]

---

[14] The scholarship on SDT has not yet created a stage development rubric that uses an SDT framework. Email to Neil Hamilton from Larry Krieger, April 6, 2021 (on file with the authors).

TABLE 22 *Milestone Model on well-being practices*

Sub-competencies of Well-Being Practices	Novice Learner (Level 1)	Intermediate Learner (Level 2)	Competent Learner (Level 3)	Exceptional Learner (Level 4)
1. Autonomy *To feel in control of the person's own goals and behaviors*	RARELY recognizes the importance of autonomy	SOMETIMES recognizes the importance of autonomy and can list resources available to increase autonomy	OFTEN recognizes the importance of autonomy and with assistance creates a plan to increase autonomy	CONSISTENTLY recognizes the importance of autonomy and independently has created a plan to increase autonomy
2. Competence *To feel the person has the needed skills to be successful*	See Table 19 outlining the sub-competencies of ownership over the student's own professional development.			
3. Relatedness *To experience a sense of belonging and attachment to other people*	See Table 20 outlining the sub-competencies of internalizing a deep responsibility and service orientation to others, especially the client, and Table 21 on the sub-competencies of client-centered problem-solving.			
	RARELY recognizes the importance of relatedness	SOMETIMES recognizes the importance of relatedness and can list resources available to increase relatedness	OFTEN recognizes the importance of relatedness and with assistance creates a plan to increase relatedness	CONSISTENTLY recognizes the importance of relatedness and independently has created a plan to increase relatedness

APPENDIX C

Further Research Needed on the Major Transitions for Law Students

Further research on the major transitions experienced by law students needs to be undertaken. The survey data in Table 17 in Chapter 4 focused on major transitions as they relate to the first of our four PD&F goals. To complete study of major transitions and their effect on that goal, the next step is to replicate this survey of rising 2Ls at other law schools and compare the results to these data. In addition, legal educators need a similar survey of the transitions in the 2L and 3L years. Table 23 lists transitions that the authors believe should be included in a survey after the summer between the 2L and the 3L years, and in a survey at the end of the 3L year. The entire process of study might then be replicated to assess major transitions that affect a student's development on the remaining three PD&F goals that are central to the formation of a law student's professional identity.

TABLE 23 *Transitions on ownership over a student's continuous professional development that should be included in a survey after the summer between the 2L and the 3L years, and a survey at the end of the 3L year*

1. All professionally authentic experiences (real-life or mimicking real-life)
    a. All work experiences, paid or unpaid, especially the summer work experiences
    b. All simulation experiences
    c. All clinic experiences
    d. Externship experiences
2. Other experiences more indirectly related to a lawyer's work
    a. Search for summer employment in the summer between the 2L and 3L years
    b. Search for postgraduation employment
    c. Leadership experience in student organizations
    d. Fall and spring final examination periods and grades
    e. Bar application
    f. Upper-level writing requirement
    g. Pro bono or volunteer hours requirements
    h. Experiences with Career and Professional Development Office

APPENDIX D

Milestone Model on Reflection and Reflection Writing Assignment Grading Template
The authors created this Milestone Model and Grading Template.

ASSESSMENT OF A STUDENT'S SKILL OF REFLECTION BASED ON A NUMBER OF EXPERIENCES WHERE THE STUDENT DID INDIVIDUAL REFLECTION WRITING ASSIGNMENTS

The skill of reflection is an ongoing cycle of careful examination of specific thoughts and actions from a student's own perspective and the perspective of others with a goal of informing and improving the student's insight and practice in future experiences.[1] This Milestone can be used to assess a student's overall skill of reflection over time based on, for example, a portfolio of individual reflection writing assignments.

---

[1] *See* Quoc D. Nguyen et al., *What Is Reflection? A Conceptual Analysis of Major Definitions and a Proposal for a Five-Component Model*, 48 MED. EDUC. 1176, 1189 (2014); Lawrence Grierson et al., *The Reliability Characteristics of the REFLECT Rubric for Assessing Reflective Capacity through Expressive Writing Assignments*, 9 PERSPECT. MED. EDUC. 281 (2020); Tony Marshall, *The Concept of Reflection: A Systematic Review and Thematic Synthesis across Professional Contexts*, 20 REFLECTIVE PRAC. 396, 411 (2019). Lindsey Gustafson made very useful suggestions on an earlier draft of this Milestone Model.

Sub-competencies of Reflection	Novice Learner (Level 1)	Intermediate Learner (Level 2)	Competent Learner (Level 3)	Exceptional Learner (Level 4)
1. In every reflection, the student identifies the specific thoughts and actions the student is examining relevant to the assignment.	RARELY identifies specific thoughts and actions the student is examining.	SOMETIMES identifies the specific thoughts and actions the student is examining.	OFTEN identifies the specific thoughts and actions the student is examining.	CONSISTENTLY identifies the specific thoughts and actions the student is examining.
2. The student carefully examines specific thoughts and actions from the student's own perspective and the perspective of others.[2]	RARELY carefully examines specific thoughts and actions from the student's own perspective and the perspectives of others.	SOMETIMES carefully examines specific thoughts and actions from the student's own perspective and the perspectives of others.	OFTEN carefully examines specific thoughts and actions from the student's own perspective and the perspectives of others.	CONSISTENTLY carefully examines specific thoughts and actions from the student's own perspective and the perspectives of others.
3. Shows awareness of the student's own conceptual framework(s) (e.g., the motivations, intentions, beliefs, premises, and values) that underlie the thoughts and actions.[3]	RARELY shows awareness of the student's own conceptual framework that underlies the thoughts and actions.	SOMETIMES shows awareness of the student's own conceptual framework that underlies the thoughts and actions.	OFTEN shows awareness of the student's own conceptual framework that underlies the thoughts and actions.	CONSISTENTLY shows awareness of the student's own conceptual framework that underlies the thoughts and actions.

[2] Note that there are three measurables here: the student's perspective, the perspectives of others, and careful examination of both.

[3] For example, is the conceptual framework principally motivating the student's thoughts and actions focused on rule compliance, rewards and recognition, compliance with social norms and expectations, internal values, or awareness of gaps in the student's current conceptual framework. This is based on constructive-developmental theory. *See* Neil Hamilton & Verna Monson, *Ethical Professional Transformation: Themes from Interviews About Professionalism with Exemplary Lawyers*, 52 SANTA CLARA L. REV. 921, 937 (2012).

(continued)

Sub-competencies of Reflection	Novice Learner (Level 1)	Intermediate Learner (Level 2)	Competent Learner (Level 3)	Exceptional Learner (Level 4)
4. Considers changes in terms of the student's conceptual framework.	RARELY considers changes in terms of the student's conceptual framework.	SOMETIMES considers changes in terms of the student's conceptual framework.	OFTEN considers changes in terms of the student's conceptual framework.	CONSISTENTLY considers changes in terms of the student's conceptual framework.
5. Engages in the above steps iteratively over time.	RARELY engages in the above steps iteratively over time.	SOMETIMES engages in the above steps iteratively over time.	OFTEN engages in the above steps iteratively over time.	CONSISTENTLY engages in the above steps iteratively over time.

* The instructor should first look over the Milestone Model on Assessment of a Student's Skill of Reflection Based on a Number of Experiences Where the Student Did Individual Reflection Writing Assignments to understand the stages of development for this competency. This grading template is for individual assignments. Note that the instructor must fill in the points to be given for each level of performance on each sub-competency depending on the total points available for the assignment

Sub-competencies of Reflection	Novice Learner (Level 1)	Intermediate Learner (Level 2)	Competent Learner (Level 3)	Exceptional Learner (Level 4)
1. Identifies the specific thoughts and actions the student is examining with respect to the experience(s) above.	Provides no narrative explaining the specific thoughts and actions the student is examining in the context of the experience(s) in the assignment.	Provides a cursory narrative explaining the specific thoughts and actions the student is examining in the context of the experience(s) in the assignment.	Provides a general narrative explaining the specific thoughts and actions the student is examining in the context of the experience(s) in the assignment.	Provides a thorough narrative explaining the specific thoughts and actions the student is examining in the context of the experience(s) in the assignment.
2. From the perspectives that the instructor has identified including the student's own perspective, the student carefully examines the specific thoughts and actions.	Examines the experience(s) only from the student's own perspective.	Examines the experience(s) largely from the student's own perspective and only considers additional perspectives the instructor has identified in a superficial manner.	Examines the experience(s) from multiple perspectives identified by the instructor, including a personal perspective, but fails to identify and examine one or more of the other important perspectives in a meaningful way.	Examines the experience(s) from multiple perspectives identified by the instructor, including a personal perspective, in a meaningful way.
3. Student shows awareness of the conceptual framework(s) (e.g., the motivations, intentions, beliefs, premises, and values) that underlie the student's thoughts and actions.[4]	Shows just surface-level awareness of the student's own conceptual framework underlying the student's thoughts and actions.	Shows some depth in awareness of the student's own conceptual framework underlying the student's thoughts and actions.	Shows significant depth in awareness of the student's own conceptual framework underlying the student's thoughts and actions.	Shows deep awareness of the student's own conceptual framework underlying the student's thoughts and actions.

[4] For example, is the conceptual framework principally motivating the student's thoughts and actions focused on rule compliance, rewards and recognition, compliance with social norms and expectations, internal values, or awareness of gaps in student's current conceptual framework. This is based on constructive-developmental theory. *See* Neil Hamilton & Verna Monson, *Ethical Professional Transformation: Themes from Interviews About Professionalism with Exemplary Lawyers*, 52 SANTA CLARA L. REV. 921, 937 (2012).

(continued)

Sub-competencies of Reflection	Novice Learner (Level 1)	Intermediate Learner (Level 2)	Competent Learner (Level 3)	Exceptional Learner (Level 4)
4. Student considers changes in the student's conceptual framework that lead to an action step(s).	Focuses only on the past with no indication how insights gained might change both student's conceptual framework and lead to an action step.	Provides some consideration of how insights gained might change student's conceptual framework and lead to an action step. Good definition of an action step.	Provides good consideration of how insights gained might change student's conceptual framework and lead to an action step. Excellent definition of an action step.	Provides in-depth consideration of how insights gained might change student's conceptual framework and lead to an action step. Outstanding definition of an action step.

REFLECTION WRITING ASSIGNMENT GRADING TEMPLATE[5]

Course Name:
Assignment Name:

_____

[For the instructor to put into the assignment.] Explain briefly the experience(s) that are the subject for this reflection assignment.

_____
_____
_____
_____
_____

[For the instructor to put into the assignment.] List the multiple perspectives that the instructor wants the student to consider with respect to the experience(s) that are the topic of the reflective writing assignment. E.g. readings, class discussion, interviews, client meeting, team discussion, student research, etc.

_____
_____
_____
_____
_____

Note that the instructor may choose to include points for the quality of the student's writing.

---

[5] This grading template adopts the four sub-competencies of a reflective thinking process defined by Quoc D. Nguyen et al. based on a systematic review of medical education scholarship. Nguyen et al., *supra* note 1, at 1182. The template also adapts some language in the descriptions of the novice, intermediate, competent, and exceptional learner stages from Prof. Kendall Kerew's Reflection Rubric. *See* email to Neil Hamilton from Kendall Kerew, Feb. 27, 2020 (on file with the authors). The template also adapts some language from the American Association of Colleges and Universities' *Foundation and Skills for Lifelong Learning VALUE Rubric*, https://www.aacu.org/value/rubrics/lifelong-learning.

5

Going Where Each Major Stakeholder Is and Building Bridges among Them in Order to Realize the Four Professional Development and Formation Goals

In Chapters 1, 2, and 3, we developed a framework that faculty, staff, and administrators can employ to bring purposeful, effective support to students in the pursuit of the four goals that are central to their professional development and formation:

- Ownership of continuous professional development toward excellence at the major competencies that clients, employers, and the legal system need;
- a deep responsibility and service orientation to others, especially the client;
- a client-centered, problem-solving approach and good judgment that ground the student's responsibility and service to the client; and
- well-being practices.

Chapter 4 built on that framework, offering ten core principles to guide and inform faculty, staff, and administrators as they undertake the work of supporting students toward the four PD&F goals. The focus was on principles that will make everything easier, more efficient, and more effective in practice.

In this chapter, we keep with the emphasis on the practical and turn attention to the very practical matter of how to proceed in a law school. Each law school is an institution with diverse stakeholders who possess differing interests. It is an institution with multiple priorities and limited resources. Like many other institutions, it can exhibit signs of resistance to change and skepticism of innovation. With those realities in mind, this chapter provides nine practical implementation suggestions. All nine are premised on the expectation that progress likely will be incremental, that interest in more purposeful support of PD&F goals will need to be cultivated, and that many in the law school community have much still to learn about professional development and formation. Behind all nine suggestions, too, is the belief that all the major stakeholders of a law school do in fact have something to gain from more purposeful support of PD&F goals. In seeking their engagement and participation, it is crucial to "go where they are" – to appreciate the perspectives, interests, and needs of each major stakeholder (faculty, staff, administrators, students, legal employers, and the legal profession itself), and to build bridges that connect stakeholders to the project of fostering each student's growth toward later stages of the four PD& F goals.

5.1 ASSESS LOCAL CONDITIONS WITH RESPECT TO THE FACULTY, STAFF, AND ADMINISTRATORS

The first practical implementation suggestion is to assess local conditions among faculty, staff, and administrators at the law school. Are any of them interested in taking even small steps to help each student develop to the next level on any of the four goals? Remember that there are many on-ramps to these four foundational PD&F goals, but the various stakeholders in the law school may need help to see how their individual interests are served by fostering each student's growth toward later stages of the four foundational goals. Law schools, in the authors' experience, are relatively "siloed." Each stakeholder tends to concentrate on a discrete area of responsibility and can be unaware of or indifferent to matters arising in another area. What are the enlightened self-interest reasons for each siloed group, framed in the language of that group, to foster student growth toward these goals?

Earlier discussion in Chapter 2 discussed the perspectives of the major internal stakeholders and how their self-interests might be served by stronger law school support of PD&F goals Here, we expand on the idea, illustrating how particular various stakeholders might identify and associate with one or another of the four PD&F goals.

The first goal – fostering each student's growth to later stages of ownership of continuous professional development toward excellence at the major competencies that clients, employers, and the legal system need – may find the greatest initial interest and support because many faculty and staff of all types are concerned about the weak levels of initiative and commitment that they discern in some of their students. Indeed, one-third of all schools have adopted an institutional learning outcome to foster each student's self-directed or self-regulated learning. Chapter 1 emphasized that student growth toward later stages of self-directed learning improves the probability of stronger academic performance, bar passage, and postgraduation employment outcomes. Chapter 4 in addition emphasized that a continuous coaching

TABLE 24 *Percentage of law schools adopting a learning outcome building on a student's internalized responsibility and service to others*

Thirty-eight percent include a learning outcome on understanding the value of providing pro bono service to the disadvantaged;
thirty-three percent include a learning outcome on teamwork/collaboration;
twenty-seven percent include a cultural competency learning outcome;
twenty-seven percent include a version of a professionalism or high ethical standards learning outcome (which is related to trustworthiness in relationships);
fifteen percent include a learning outcome on integrity (which also relates to trustworthiness in relationships);
thirteen percent include a learning outcome on interviewing, counseling or both;
twelve percent include a learning outcome on active listening;
six percent include a learning outcome on respect for others;
six percent include a learning outcome on leadership; and
five percent include a learning outcome on client-centered problem-solving.

model is the most effective curriculum to foster this type of student growth while also serving diversity, equity, and inclusion (DEI) and Belonging goals by increasing historically underserved students' sense of belonging and general student well-being. Improved outcomes on these fronts should prove attractive to many faculty, staff, and administrators, paving the way to interest in promoting PD&F goals. Podium faculty, on the other hand, should see that later stage growth on this learning outcome promotes achievement of the cognitive goals that podium faculty set for students. Even if podium faculty are not ready to incorporate the first PD&F goal in their own teaching, they might at least endorse its importance and give "cross-selling" support to its pursuit elsewhere in the law school, signaling to students that the goal needs to be taken seriously.

With respect to the second goal – fostering each student's growth toward later stages of a deep responsibility and service orientation to others, especially the client – many faculty, staff, and administrators may agree that a fiduciary mindset or disposition is important. They may, however, find the goal too abstract or be skeptical that legal education can foster this type of growth. It may help if they see a more concrete learning outcome that builds on a deep responsibility and service orientation to others, especially the client. Chapter 4 emphasized that significant numbers of law schools have adopted learning outcomes that rest upon this foundation. Table 24 indicates the percentage of law schools that have adopted institutional learning outcomes that are sub-competencies related to this second goal.

Where the faculty has adopted any of these learning outcomes (e.g., pro bono service, cultural competency, teamwork/collaboration), the faculty and staff most interested in that outcome will be a promising group to support further steps. Given societal challenges regarding racial justice, for instance, there may be faculty, staff, and administrators drawn particularly toward fostering each student's growth toward later stages of pro bono service to the disadvantaged and access to justice or to cultural competency. Perhaps faculty and staff interested in DEI and Belonging or student well-being might see that learning outcomes relating to building relationships and intrinsic meaning will promote student belonging and well-being.

The third PD&F goal – fostering a client-centered problem-solving approach and good judgment that ground each student's responsibility and service to the client – links the general fiduciary mindset and disposition language of the second goal to the specific competencies that clients and legal employers want. Some faculty and staff – particularly those who are concerned with student readiness for practice and success in the employment market – may find this an appealing bridge. It connects legal doctrine and legal analysis to their concerns in the form of client-centered problem solving and good judgment.

The fourth PD&F goal – helping each student to internalize well-being practices – will be of great interest to faculty and staff focused on student stress and anxiety, depression, and substance abuse. As we discussed in Chapter 1, there are important links between Goal 1 (internalizing a commitment to continuous professional development), Goal 2 (internalizing a deep responsibility and service orientation to others), and the basic psychological needs that contribute to well-being.

5.2 BUILD A "COALITION OF THE WILLING"

A second practical implementation suggestion is to build a "coalition of the willing" who want to help move the school forward in fostering student growth on any of the four PD&F goals (or any of their sub-competencies). In the initial period of experimentation, focus on gradual small steps that the coalition can try, and keep the faculty informed. The authors' experience indicates that success can be had with small "pilot projects" that take advantage of the substantial autonomy that professors have in their courses and hence may not require formal approval. Suppose, for instance, that the coalition of the willing includes all the professors who teach a particular required course. These faculty members are well positioned to experiment with a formation-oriented pedagogy that all students might thus experience. Professors teaching courses in a distance-learning format might find a pilot project attractive, as teamwork and team projects lend themselves well to the online learning environment and provide means for students to form relationships; build community; and develop teamwork, collaboration, and communication competencies. Interested faculty and staff might try a pilot project focused on a continuous coaching model (outlined in Chapter 4) for (1) historically underserved students to increase their sense of belonging and in turn their academic and postgraduation success, (2) students most at risk of bar examination failure to foster their growth to later stages of self-directed learning and thus higher probabilities of bar passage, or (3) students identified by academic support as needing help regarding their well-being.

It is important to focus on small, gradual steps and choose pilot projects that are both practicable and have a good probability of success given local conditions. If possible, postpone initiatives that require a faculty vote until after there have been several successful pilot projects so proponents from the coalition of the willing can share their positive experiences with their colleagues. Those colleagues may come to embrace purposeful law school support of PD&F goals, but they must first become acquainted with the innovation and hear of its practicality and its benefits.[1]

5.3 BUILD A LEARNING COMMUNITY OF FACULTY AND STAFF INTERESTED IN ANY OF THE FOUR PD&F GOALS

This practical implementation suggestion builds on the idea of a coalition of the willing with a next step: the creation of a learning community. A faculty and staff learning community regularly discusses how most effectively to foster each student's growth toward later stages of the four PD&F goals.[2] The learning community can provide feedback to individual faculty and staff members regarding curriculum ideas, break down the silos among faculty and staff, and become a source for information that can help other faculty and staff grow in their appreciation of the positive benefits and feasibility of supporting PD&F goals.

---

[1] *See* Louis D. Bilionis, *Law School Leadership and Leadership Development for Developing Lawyers*, 58 Santa Clara L. Rev. 601, 612–631 (2018) (examining professional identity formation support as an "innovation" subject to Everett M. Rogers' theory of the diffusion of innovations); *see generally* Everett M. Rogers, Diffusion of Innovations (1962) (3d ed. 1983).

[2] *See* David Gomillion et al., *Learning How to Teach: The Case for Faculty Learning Communities*, 18 Inform. Systems Educ. J. 74–79 (2020).

Medical education's experience is that one-time faculty development interventions are not as robust in impact as longitudinal interventions. It is beneficial whenever possible to have ongoing faculty and staff development where participants share successes, discuss challenges, learn new skills, and recalibrate.[3] Learning communities at individual schools can reach out to learning communities at other schools that are working on the same learning outcomes.

Learning communities also can be the laboring oars on curricular change over time – including the taking of the gradual steps that can evolve into a coordinated progression of modules in the curriculum on a specific PD&F goal. The traditional law school committee that addresses curriculum development tends to perform a reactive function, reacting to faculty proposals regarding courses at a course level. As Steven Bahls points out, "[i]f curricular decisions are made primarily at the course level, students do not have sufficient assurance that they will have opportunities to achieve the overall outcomes necessary to prepare them to be responsible members of the profession."[4] To move the curriculum over time toward a coordinated, sequenced progression of modules on a PD&F goal, the law school should have a proactive committee of faculty and staff members with on-the-ground understanding of that PD&F goal as it applies in the school.

5.4 ALWAYS "GO WHERE THEY ARE" WITH RESPECT TO FACULTY, STAFF, AND ADMINISTRATORS

A fourth practical implementation suggestion borrows from Principle 3 in Chapter 4 – the principle that you should go where they are with students; take into account that students are at different developmental stages of growth on PD&F goals; and, accordingly, engage each student at the student's present developmental stage. It is wise to extend the same concept to faculty, staff, and administrators. A faculty member who has never experienced strong professional development and formation teaching or excellent guided reflection with a coach might think, for example, that any curriculum involving the four PD&F goals will require stand-up lectures on philosophy and ethics. Other faculty might hear "professional development" and think the topic is about "jobs," "resume-crafting," and "vocationalism" or about civility, dress codes,

---

[3] Jennifer Kogan & Eric Holmboe, *Direct Observation, in* ERIC HOLMBOE ET AL, EVALUATION OF CLINICAL COMPETENCE (2d ed. 2018) at 61, 79.

[4] Steven Bahls, *Adoption of Student Learning Outcomes: Lessons for Systemic Change in Legal Education,* 67 J. LEGAL EDUC. 376, 381 (2018).

and injunctions against Rambo litigation tactics, and thus not worth serious academic or curricular attention.

It is important to listen and understand how faculty, staff, and administrator colleagues are "hearing" any discussion of these four foundational PD&F goals and related curricular steps. It may take repeated effort over time to clarify and develop understanding about the concepts in Chapters 1 through 4. If possible, "visit" one-on-one with faculty and staff to draw out and clarify what they are hearing and understanding. Doing so may reveal that some faculty and staff are drawn toward one PD&F goal, while others are drawn toward a different one. It also may suggest opportunities to better inform faculty and staff of the nature of professional identity formation and the ways that they and the law school can support student development.[5]

With respect to faculty and staff who have little or no interest in these four PD&F goals, keep them informed. An "ask" of their time and energy in direct support of professional identity formation efforts might be unadvisable. But some may be willing, sooner or eventually later, to spend a few minutes with their students "cross-selling" the importance of the PD&F curriculum for the students' future. Provide them a script of talking points to make matters easier and the cross-selling more effective.

5.5 REPEATEDLY EMPHASIZE THE VALUE AND IMPORTANCE OF "CURATING"

A fifth practical implementation suggestion is to repeatedly emphasize the concept of "curating" that was discussed in Chapter 2. There, we called for faculty and staff, in an enterprise-wide effort, to "curate" the experiences and environments that promote each student's growth toward later stages of the four PD&F goals. This means connecting the experiences and environments to one another in an intelligently sequenced fashion, and guiding the students through them with a framework that helps each student understand the student's own development through the process. Curating produces a more cogent program for students while using the law school's resources more efficiently and effectively. Faculty can play a lead role in the design of the experiences and environments while coordinating with staff who have responsibility for some of the modules in an enterprise-wide curriculum. For

---

[5] For example, Prof. Christy DeSanctis at George Washington University School of Law, in trying to convince the faculty to add two credits on PD&F goals to a required 1L lawyering skills curriculum, found that many faculty responded most favorably to PD&F Goal 4 – client-centered problem solving. December 8, 2019, email from Christy DeSanctis to Neil Hamilton (on file with the authors).

example, a law school that has adopted a teamwork/collaboration learning outcome will want both faculty and staff who are advisors of student organizations like the law journal, the various competitions involving teams, and student government to work together to foster each student's growth toward later stages on teamwork skills. Similarly, if a law school is emphasizing support to each student who is at some risk of failing the bar to grow to later stages of self-directed learning, the faculty, the academic support staff, and the dean of students will work together to do this.

As we noted in Chapter 2, a law school can improve its support of the four PD&F goals with an enterprise-wide curating strategy even if it declines to adopt competency-based education as its educational model. Chapters 3 and 4, which borrow from medical education's twenty years of additional experience with competency-based education, present concepts that will be useful in an enterprise-wide curating strategy even if the law school is not embracing competency-based education. A school that declines to formally establish a Milestone Model as discussed in Chapter 4 might nonetheless discuss and reflect on what milestones might be associated with a specific learning outcome. Discussion and agreement on the stages of development would be extremely useful in conceptualizing how to curate useful experiences and environments for students that support their progress.

5.6 RECOGNIZE THE SCOPE OF THE CHALLENGE IN FOSTERING A SHARED UNDERSTANDING AMONG FACULTY, STAFF, AND ADMINISTRATORS ABOUT THE STAGES OF STUDENT DEVELOPMENT ON COMPETENCIES BEYOND THOSE MOST FAMILIAR TO LAW SCHOOLS. FOCUS ON GRADUAL SMALL STEPS TAILORED TO LOCAL CONDITIONS

If legal education's experience over the next twenty years is similar to medical education's earlier two decades of experience with learning outcomes like the four foundational PD&F goals this book emphasizes, then a sixth practical implementation suggestion stands out. Be aware of the scope of the challenge, and focus on gradual small steps each year tailored to local conditions.

The biggest challenge for medical education has been that medical faculty and staff historically have not had a clear shared understanding (a shared mental model or mental representation) about

1. How the capacities, skills, and values beyond the traditional technical medical skills are defined;

2. how students develop through stages toward a defined level of competence at these other capacities, skills, and values; and

3. what curricular engagements are most effective to foster each student's growth toward later stages of these other capacities, skills, and values.[6]

Milestone Models, discussed in Chapter 3, proved to be a beneficial way for medical education to tackle the challenge and create clear shared understanding among faculty and staff.[7] When faculty, staff, and administrators – the coalition of the willing – select a specific competency included in the four PD&F goals and come to some agreement on students' stages of development, they not only achieve a clear, shared understanding of the competency but also lay the groundwork for curating the environment and experiences of the students to foster student growth. Proceeding from common ground, they also will be moving toward some inter-rater reliability in assessment of the competency.

5.7 EMPHASIZE THAT THERE ARE MANY SUCCESSFUL EXAMPLES THAT CAN BE FOLLOWED OR ADAPTED TO FOSTER STUDENT GROWTH TOWARD LATER STAGES OF THE FOUR PD&F GOALS – AND DRAW FROM THEM

A seventh practical implementation suggestion is to emphasize to faculty and staff that there are many other law schools and groups working to foster student growth toward the four foundational PD&F goals and many successful examples of curriculum that could be built upon to fit local conditions. As the examples and sources discussed next illustrate, interested faculty and staff hardly need to start from scratch. Models and guides are available to make initiative practicable, easy to execute, efficient, compatible with one's practices and values, and likely to succeed – the criteria that make it easier for people to change and innovate.[8] What follow here are just a few examples that show the wide range of models, ideas, and initiatives from which a law school might draw.

---

[6] Eric Holmboe et al., *Mastery Learning, Milestones, and Entrustable Professional Activities*, in COMPREHENSIVE HEALTHCARE SIMULATION: MASTERY LEARNING IN HEALTH PROFESSIONS EDUCATION at 314, 323–25 (W. McGaghie et al., eds. 2020).

[7] *Id.* at 314–15.

[8] *See* Bilionis, *supra* note 1, at 612–16. For example, Scott Fruewald has a number of useful professional identity exercises in his book, HOW TO GROW A LAWYER 163–94 (2018). Fruehwald also has many useful reflection questions on professional identity and self-regulated learning in his book, DEVELOPING YOUR PROFESSIONAL IDENTITY: CREATING YOUR INNER LAWYER 1–39 (2015).

5.7.1 A Milestone Model on the Goal/Learning Outcome That Is of Most Interest Given Local Conditions

Faculty and staff may have a shared – although perhaps unwritten and unspoken – mental model of the stages of student development regarding the standard law school competencies of knowledge of doctrinal law, legal analysis, and legal research and writing. But they likely do not share an understanding of progressive stages of growth on the four PD&F goals and their sub-competencies, such as teamwork, pro bono service, or cross-cultural competency. For the reasons outlined in Chapters 3 and 4, it is important to strive for a shared mental model of the students' stages of development on these learning outcomes. Articulating a Milestone Model on even a single competency – for instance, on ownership over a student's own professional development (self-directed learning) – can help move faculty and staff toward shared understanding. It also can serve as a direct measure of assessment for accreditation purposes (Principle 10 in Chapter 4), with faculty and staff observing and assessing each student's stage of development using the Milestone Model (Principle 8 in Chapter 4 on multi-source observation and assessment).

Models are available. Responding to the most common learning outcomes that law schools have been adopting, the Holloran Center organized national working groups of faculty and staff to create stage-development Milestone Models on self-directed learning, teamwork, cross-cultural competency, integrity, and honoring commitments as part of professionalism.[9] Other stage-development models have been reported in the scholarly literature.[10] Milestone Models for PD&F Goals 1, 2, 3, and 4 also may be found in Appendix B to Chapter 4.

5.7.2 A Required PD&F Curriculum in the 1L Year

A fast-growing number of law schools (more than sixty – almost a third of all law schools) are now requiring professional development and formation curriculum in the 1L year to respond to concerns about bar passage,

---

[9] The Holloran Milestone Models can be found at www.stthomas.edu/hollorancenter/holloran competencymilestones/. The center has national working groups creating Milestone Models on pro bono service commitments, active listening, leadership, and professional communication available on the center's website in spring 2022..

[10] *See, e.g.,* Andrea Curcio, *A Simple Low-Cost Institutional Learning Outcome Assessment Model,* 67 J. LEGAL EDUC. 489–530 (2018) (discussing stage development models used at Georgia State University College of Law).

postgraduation employment outcomes, and student well-being.[11] The learning outcomes for these new required 1L professional development and formation initiatives tend to pursue two principal themes: (1) developing and demonstrating self-understanding, self-direction, and discernment of the student's path in the legal market and (2) developing and demonstrating the relationship and communication skills needed in the legal market.[12] These track closely with the first two foundational PD&F learning outcomes (ownership of continuous professional development toward excellence at the major competencies that clients, employers, and the legal system need and a deep responsibility and service orientation to others, especially the client).

A recent example is the University of Richmond School of Law's one-credit required course in the 1L year. The course's learning outcomes emphasize (1) discerning the student's own values as a member of the legal profession; (2) developing critical interpersonal lawyering skills; and (3) engaging in self-directed learning, including designing and implementing a written plan for ongoing professional development and well-being.[13] An example of a longer-standing required initiative is the University of St. Thomas School of Law's Mentor Externship, which emphasizes (1) fostering the highest levels of professionalism; (2) developing the relationship skills necessary for professional success in any employment context; and (3) deepening and broadening each student's professional competencies, emphasizing self-directed learning.[14]

Required PD&F offerings that award credit hours have emphasized reflection exercises, simulations, group discussions, and some panel presentations.[15] Required courses that afford no credit hours most commonly have featured panel presentations and lectures. Several use self-assessments of some sort, and many also employ a mock interview.[16]

These efforts to foster student guided reflection and self-awareness of strengths are in keeping with Principle 4 in Chapter 4 (stressing the importance of guided reflection to foster growth on the PD&F learning outcomes). They also model Principle 7 (urging law schools to help each student

---

[11] See Jerome Organ, *Common Threads Across Increasingly Common First-Year Courses/Programs Focused on Professional Development*, PROF. DEV. Q. (Feb. 2020) at 20, 21.

[12] *Id.* at 21–24.

[13] Email to Neil W. Hamilton from Janice Craft, the new director of the Richmond program, on July 8, 2020 (on file with the authors).

[14] See Mentor Externship Program, https://www.stthomas.edu/law/practicaltraining/mentor/).

[15] See Organ, *supra* note 11 at 20, 22–25.

[16] *Id.*

understand how new knowledge, skills, and capacities are building upon the student's existing experience and strengths to achieve the student's goals).

5.7.3 A Requirement That Each Student Create and Implement a Written Professional Development Plan with Coaching Feedback (the ROADMAP Curriculum)

The ROADMAP curriculum[17] is designed to help each student create a written professional development plan with coaching feedback starting in January or February of the 1L year and then implement the plan throughout the remaining time in law school. The objective is to better realize the student's goals of bar passage and meaningful postgraduation employment. The ROADMAP steps are specifically designed to assist a student's growth to later stages of development on (1) ownership over the student's own professional development (self-directed learning); (2) a deep responsibility and service orientation to others, especially the client; and (3) a client-centered problem-solving approach and good judgment.[18] Student growth to later stages of the first two ROADMAP goals should contribute to student well-being as discussed in Chapter 1.

---

[17] Neil W. Hamilton, ROADMAP: The Law Student's Guide to Meaningful Employment (2d ed. 2018).

[18] Data support the importance of an initiative along the lines of the ROADMAP curriculum. First- year student self-assessment of their stage of development on self-directed learning at six law schools indicates that more than 40 percent of the students are self-assessing at an earlier stage of development on self-directed learning, although data from two of the schools that 70 percent of the 1L student respondents either had no written plan at all or were just beginning to write a plan indicate a very substantial social desirability bias. *See* Larry Natt Gantt II & Benjamin Madison, *Self-Directedness and Professional Formation: Connecting Two Critical Concepts in Legal Education*, 14 U. St. Thomas L. J. 498, 498, 503–08 (2018). Three years of student self-assessment at the University of St. Thomas Law School indicate that prior to completing the ROADMAP curriculum and receiving feedback from a coach, 57.4 percent of the students were self-assessing at one of the two earlier stages of self-directed learning (with 6.8 percent assessing themselves in the earliest stage). After completing the ROADMAP curriculum and receiving feedback from a coach, only 8.7 percent were self-assessing at one of the two earlier stages of self-directed learning (with none assessing themselves in the earliest stage). *See* Neil Hamilton, *Professional Formation with Emerging Adult Law Students in the 21–29 Age Group: Engaging Law Students to Take Ownership of Their Own Professional Development Toward Both Excellence and Meaningful Employment*, 2015 J. of the Prof. Lawyer 125, 143–44.

Former North Carolina law dean and president of the American Association of Law Schools, Judith Welch Wegner, covered the strengths of the ROADMAP curriculum in a book review. *See* Judith Welch Wegner, *Book Review: ROADMAP: The Law Student's Guide to Meaningful Employment* (2d ed. 2018), 68 J. Legal Educ. 184–190 (2019).

Coaching is an important element of the ROADMAP curriculum. Each student has a one-on-one meeting for forty-five to sixty minutes with a coach who provides feedback and encourages guided reflection. One of the coauthors, Professor Hamilton, has been organizing coaches for individual meetings with roughly 160 1L students each year since 2013. His experience indicates that many doctrinal faculty may be not well suited to the coaching role, as they lack significant, recent experience in law practice and also are unaccustomed to providing the kind of attentive listening that good coaching requires. The best coaches have tended to be alumni in practice, about five to ten years out of law school, who are excellent listeners and who have experienced good coaching themselves. The Holloran Center has a coaching guide included in the Appendix to this chapter and is working on an online training program for coaches that should be available in summer 2022.

The University of St. Thomas School of Law has recently extended the ROADMAP coaching model and begun assigning the best internal coaches among faculty and staff to the students most at risk of not passing the bar exam (based on 1L fall semester grades). This is a continuous coaching model over each student's remaining two and a half years of law school. There is not yet data on whether this program is increasing bar passage probabilities for this group.

ABA Publications, the publisher of the ROADMAP, is publishing *Critical Lawyering Skills: A Companion Guide to the ROADMAP*, by Thiadora Pina, Laura Jacobus, and Rupa Bandari. This book approaches the ROADMAP learning outcomes through a lawyering skills framework with excellent reflective exercises each week for the student. The *Companion Guide* also has a *Professor's Manual*.

The ROADMAP curriculum, with a coach or a faculty member using the coaching guide in Appendix E to this chapter or the *Companion Guide*, applies the following principles from Chapter 4 – Principle 3 (go where the students are), Principle 4 (on repeated opportunities for guided reflection and self-assessment), Principle 5 (on the importance of coaching), Principle 6 (on coaching at the key transition points of law school), Principle 7 (on helping the student see how new knowledge, skills, and capacities are helping the student achieve their goals and building on existing strengths and experiences), and Principle 10 (on the importance of direct measures that an observer, such as a coach, can employ to assess the student's stage of development on a Milestone Model). The continuous coaching model for at-risk students regarding bar passage also can lead to the creation of portfolios for each student, meeting Principle 9.

5.7.4 A 1L *Constitutional Law Curriculum That Also Fosters Student Professional Development and Formation*

One of the coauthors, Professor Bilionis, has incorporated a PD&F objective into a basic required first-year course in constitutional law. In addition to traditional competencies, the course explicitly spotlights collaboration and teamwork. The course's stated learning objectives include the student's ability to "participate as a member of a professional community whose members work individually and together to continuously improve their capacities to serve clients and society." (This is a community of practice as discussed in Principle 6 in Chapter 4.) From the outset and throughout the course, the significance of a broad range of competencies to successful law practice is emphasized. The value of collaboration and teamwork to the student's own learning while in law school also is stressed.

Each student is randomly assigned to a team for the entire semester. In every class session, one or more teams is "on call" to be exceptionally well prepared to explore the assigned reading as well as a distributed problem that places students in contexts they will encounter in practice. The teams regularly confer prior to class, using whatever means they choose (face-to-face, Zoom, or asynchronously in writing). Also associated with every class is a short writing assignment that all students, within their teams, must undertake. Each student drafts a short response to a prompt provided by the professor and posts that response to the team's own online discussion board. The team then reviews its postings and produces a response on behalf of the entire team, capturing the best insights from its members' postings. These team responses are shared with the entire class.

Twice during the semester, the students are assigned a more substantial writing project – two memoranda that serve as capstones to two major portions of the course. The students share their own drafts with teammates, and each student is responsible for providing written feedback to a teammate during the drafting process. A third writing assignment – drafting of an answer to a practice examination – capstones another segment of the course. Students share their draft answers with the team, which then confers to reflect on the strengths of various answers, opportunities for improvement, and strategies for exam preparation and exam taking. In class, each team delivers an oral report on its discussions and reflections.

The foregoing writing assignments are assessed, with feedback provided to the team and also individually to each student. The team-based activities are graded as well, producing a grade for the team (with each team member receiving the same grade) that figures, along with the final examination, into a student's final grade in the course.[19]

Students report that the team experiences assist them in better learning the doctrinal material and advancing their analytical abilities. They also report that the team experiences contribute positively to their confidence and their appreciation of diversity. They relate that the experiences reinforce for them that all their classmates have strengths; that no one has all the answers and insights; that all have valuable perspectives to offer; and that their own individual development is strengthened by collaboration, feedback, and reflection. In the professor's opinion, students have shown improved performance on the final examination.

The structure of the course reflects several of the principles from Chapter 4. Students see a Teamwork and Team Leadership Milestone Model and do a self-assessment using the model reflecting Principle 1. There are repeated opportunities for reflection emphasized by Principle 4. The team assignments and the teamwork needed to do them simulate practice and are authentic professional experiences as contemplated by Principle 6. By resorting to extensive peer feedback in addition to feedback and assessment from the professor, the course also draws on Principle 8's acknowledgment of the potential of multi-observer feedback and assessment.

5.7.5 *A 1L Required Course on the Legal Profession*

A course at the Mercer University School of Law – "The Legal Profession" – presents another example of the possibilities with a 1L required course. The nature of the course is well captured in the textbook used in the course, authored by Patrick Emery Longan, Daisy Hurst Floyd, and Timothy W. Floyd and titled THE FORMATION OF PROFESSIONAL IDENTITY: THE PATH FROM STUDENT TO LAWYER.[20] The authors urge the student reader to be intentionally proactive about the formation of the student's professional

---

[19] A detailed syllabus of the course and its features is available on the Holloran Center's website. *See* https://www.stthomas.edu/hollorancenter/roadmap/

[20] For a review of this book, see Neil Hamilton, *Fostering Growth from Being a Student to Being a Lawyer: A Review of* THE FORMATION OF PROFESSIONAL IDENTITY: THE PATH FROM STUDENT TO Lawyer (2020), 69 J. LEGAL EDUC. 224 (2019). Note that a required leadership course is another pathway to fostering student growth toward PD&F goals. See, for instance, the new leadership textbook, LEAH W. TEAGUE, ELIZABETH FRALEY, & STEPHEN RISPOLI, FUNDAMENTALS OF LAWYER LEADERSHIP (2021).

identity (defined as an individual with a "deep sense of self in a particular role" who can answer the question "I am the kind of law student/lawyer who _____") and to internalize the traditional core values of the profession into the student's existing value system.[21]

The authors define the traditional core values of the legal profession in terms of virtues – capacities or dispositions that bring a person closer to an ideal.[22] They argue that there is substantial consensus in the profession about "the virtues necessary to be the kind of lawyer who serves clients well and helps fulfill the public purposes of the profession"[23] and set out six professional virtues that the student should internalize into their existing value system to form a professional identity:[24]

1. The virtue of competence;
2. the virtue of fidelity to the client;
3. the virtue of fidelity to the law;
4. the virtue of public spiritedness;
5. the virtue of civility; and
6. the virtue of practical wisdom (the master virtue).

The authors analyze each of the six virtues in similarly structured separate chapters that

1. Define the meaning of the virtue in the context of the Model Rules of Professional Conduct and the needs of clients, legal employers, and the profession;
2. explain what gets in the way of the lawyer's developing and demonstrating the virtue;
3. offer strategies for cultivating the virtue;
4. provide discussion questions and problems; and
5. supply suggested readings.

The structure of the book reflects several of the best empirically researched principles for an effective curriculum fostering the formation of each student's professional identity set forth earlier in Chapter 4. Consistent with Principle 4, it provides repeated opportunities for reflection on the responsibilities of the profession and development of the habit of reflective self-assessment on these

---

[21] LONGAN ET AL, THE FORMATION OF PROFESSIONAL IDENTITY: THE PATH FROM STUDENT TO LAWYER (2020), at 3–4.
[22] *Id.* at 5.
[23] *Id.*
[24] *Id.* at 5–8.

responsibilities.[25] In the same vein, the book uses problems and discussion questions at the end of each chapter that create cognitive dissonance to challenge the student's existing ideas and assumptions at the student's current stage of development.[26] Modeling Principle 7, the authors provide instruction that helps each student understand how the curriculum is helping the student achieve their goals.[27]

5.7.6 *A PD&F Curriculum Development Resource to Be Published in 2022*

Kelly Terry, Kendall Kerew, and Jerry Organ are authoring a book forthcoming in 2022, titled BECOMING LAWYERS: AN INTEGRATED APPROACH TO PROFESSIONAL IDENTITY FORMATION. The book is a resource for faculty and staff who are developing curriculum and assessment modules to foster student growth toward professional development and formation learning outcomes. Chapters of the book will cover (1) definitions of professional identity; (2) communicating the importance of professional identity formation; (3) assessing learning outcomes relating to professional identity; (4) incorporating professional identity into admissions and orientation; (5) incorporating professional identity into the 1L year; (6) incorporating professional identity into the 2L year; (7) incorporating professional identity into the 3L year; and (8) professional identity at graduation, the bar examination, and beyond.

5.8 GO WHERE THE STUDENTS ARE TO BUILD A BRIDGE FROM THEIR PERSONAL GOALS TO THE COMPETENCIES THAT CLIENTS, LEGAL EMPLOYERS, AND THE PROFESSION NEED

Our eighth practical implementation suggestion, as well as the ninth that follows, concerns the importance of communicating the relevance and significance of PD&F curriculum features to stakeholders who have a natural interest in their success. The objective is to connect the stakeholders to the school's PD&F efforts by bridging the self-interest of the stakeholders to the

---

[25] *See also* Neil Hamilton & Jerome Organ, *Thirty Reflection Questions to Help Each Student Find Meaningful Employment and Develop an Integrated Professional Identity (Professional Formation)*, 83 TENN. L. REV. 843, 868 (2016).

[26] *See also id.* at 874.

[27] *See also* Neil Hamilton, *The Next Steps of a Formation-Of-Student-Professional-Identity Social Movement: Building Bridges Among the Three Key Stakeholders – Faculty and Staff, Students, and Legal Employers and Clients*, 14 U. ST. THOMAS L. J. 285, 299–300 (2018).

values and objectives served by PD&F goals. With connection comes greater motivation to engage and participate.

We appropriately begin here with students. Students have personal goals that bear a close relation to the competencies that clients, legal employers, and the profession report that they need and want in lawyers. To maximize student "buy in" and engagement with the PD&F curriculum, a law school will do well to meet students where they are and communicate the connection between the students' own goals and PD&F competencies early, often, consistently, and in terms that students appreciate. The aim is for students to see that their own goals and PD&F competencies are conceptually related, and that the curriculum bridges them together and meaningfully promotes their advancement.

5.8.1 *What Are the Students' Goals?*

We have reasonably good data on the goals of both applicants to law school and enrolled law students. The 2018 Association of American Law Schools (AALS) report, *Before the JD: Undergraduate Views on Law School*, is the first large-scale national study to examine what factors contribute to an undergraduate student's decision to go to law school.[28] The AALS study is based on responses from 22,189 undergraduate students from 25 four-year institutions and 2,727 law students from 44 law schools.[29] The survey asked the undergraduates "how important are each of these characteristics to you when thinking about selecting a career?" The top seven characteristics that undergraduate students considering law school (and including, therefore, those selecting a law career) thought were "extremely important" are

1. Potential for career advancement – 62 percent;
2. opportunities to be helpful to others or useful to society/giving back – 54 percent;
3. ability to have a work-life balance – 50 percent;
4. advocate for social change – 37 percent;
5. potential to earn a lot of money – 31 percent;
6. opportunities to be original and creative/innovative – 27 percent; and
7. whether the job has high prestige/status – 22 percent.[30]

[28] Association of American Law Schools, Before the JD: Undergraduate Views on Law School (2018).
[29] *Id.* at 5.
[30] *Id.* at 29 fig.1.2.

A synthesis of the AALS data indicates the most important goal of undergraduate students considering law school is meaningful postgraduation employment with the potential for career advancement that "fits" the passion, motivating interests, and strengths of the student and offers a service career that is helpful to others and has some work/life balance. Achieving a high income is an additional key factor defining the meaningfulness of employment for about 30 percent of the students considering law school.[31]

5.8.2 *What Are the Competencies That Clients, Legal Employers, and the Profession Need?*

We also have reasonably good data on the competencies that clients and legal employers want. Chapter 1 and the Appendix to Chapter 1 outlined the data available and provided a Foundational Competencies Model discussed in Chapter 1 that we present again here for convenience in Figure 6.

Legal education's signature pedagogy – the case-dialogue method that dominates the first year of law school – emphasizes the cognitive skills of knowledge of doctrinal law and legal analysis, while legal writing and research, and to some degree legal judgment, also figure prominently in the standard law school curriculum.[32] These are the traditional technical competencies that law schools emphasize, as shown in Figure 6. Historically, the large majority of law schools have not had required curriculum to ensure each student's attainment of a level of competence at the other capacities and skills on the upper two sides of Figure 6. As we have noted, however, the picture in law schools is changing. A significant number of law schools have recently adopted institutional learning outcomes that include capacities and skills beyond the traditional technical competencies. Medical education once subscribed to the view that new physicians would be fine so long as they were "really smart," but it came to realize that this view was insufficient to

---

[31] Of the undergraduate students considering law school, 31 percent responded that the potential to earn a lot of money was an important characteristic in selecting a law career and 31 percent responded that "there are high-paying jobs in the field" was an extremely important or important criterion for selecting the specific law schools to which they applied. *Id.* at 44.

   Another 2017 empirical study of enrolled 1L students in five law schools asked, "What are the professional goals you would like to achieve by six months after graduation?" The two most important goals were bar passage and meaningful employment, followed by sufficient income to meet loan obligations, a satisfactory living. and a trustworthy reputation. *See* Gantt & Madison, *supra* note 18, at 503–04.

[32] William M. Sullivan et al., Educating Lawyers: Preparation for the Profession of Law 24, 50–60 (2007).

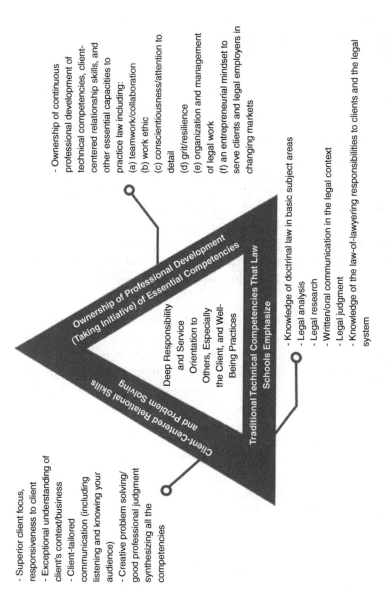

FIGURE 6 Foundational Competencies Model based on empirical studies of the competencies clients and legal employers need

meet patient and health care system needs.[33] The data on the learning outcomes that law schools are adopting indicate that legal education is coming to a similar realization of its own. Technical knowledge and cognitive skills are necessary but not sufficient to the effective practice of law. A much broader framework of capacities and skills for client-centered service is essential to meet client, legal employer, and legal system needs.

5.8.3 *Building a Bridge of Coordinated Curricular Modules to Connect the Students' Goals to Client, Legal Employer, and the Profession's Needs*

The law school's PD&F curriculum can be envisioned as a bridge that unites the students' goals of bar passage and meaningful postgraduation employment and the needs of clients, legal employers, and the legal system. Students who embrace that vision can "buy into" and engage in the curriculum more effectively. The law school can take two basic steps that will help students embrace that vision. Both steps draw upon the school's capacity to communicate well and with appreciation of the student's perspective.

The first step is to help the student envision and comprehend the bridge. Faculty, staff, and the administration can assist the student to understand

1. The full array of competencies that clients and legal employers want (this includes not only the traditional technical competencies in Figure 6 that all law schools emphasize but also other competencies in Figure 6 related to client-centered problem solving and good judgment and an entrepreneurial mindset to serve clients and legal employers in changing markets that flow from internalizing deep responsibilities to others, especially the client); and

2. The importance of a student proactively taking ownership of the student's own professional development, using both the formal curriculum and professional experiences outside of the formal curriculum, to develop toward later stages of the competencies that are the student's strengths, and to have evidence of the student's later stage development that legal employers will value.

The second step for the law school is to communicate to students, in language and with concepts that they understand, how most effectively to use the bridge that the law school's curriculum and culture create for each

---

[33]   Robert Englander, Eric Holmboe et al., *Coproducing Health Professions Education: A Prerequisite to Coproducing Health Care Services*, 95 ACAC. MED. 1006, 1007 (2020).

student. We cannot state enough the importance of Principle 3 from Chapter 4: Go Where They Are. Take into account that students are at different developmental stages with respect to the two key steps just noted.

The authors' experience is that many students need substantially more help than might be expected to grow to understand the bridge and to become proactive in using their time in law school to achieve their post-graduation goals. A number of factors appear to contribute to the difficulty. Many students want to be told what to do, a posture consistent with how they experienced their education before law school. As William Henderson has noted, law students expect to learn about their law school subjects in standard ways. The emphasis of the 1L year curriculum on cognitive competencies, moreover, means that students go relatively unexposed to the fact that the practice of law calls for a much broader array of competencies than the knowledge of legal doctrine and the performance of legal analysis.[34] As noted earlier in the discussion of Principle 3 in Chapter 4, many students also are at an earlier stage of development on self-directed learning, and they are inexperienced at purposive planning of their development as a professional.[35] Indeed, the authors' experience is that nearly all students, including highly ranked students, need substantial help in framing an effective persuasive argument for themselves that their strengths meet a particular employer's needs (in the language of the employer) and that the student has evidence of this later stage development that the employer will value.

The law school's curriculum and culture, from orientation through the remaining three years, can be used more effectively to help each student see and use the bridge, meeting them where they individually are developmentally. One powerful step in this direction would be for as many faculty as possible from all roles and ranks, whether doctrinal/podium or experiential, to make transparent to students the entire map of competencies needed to practice law, and to make explicit what competencies the student is learning in the course or in a particular experience. All faculty can emphasize the importance of the habits of seeking feedback and reflecting (Principle 4 in Chapter 4). This is particularly important, as Principle 6 in Chapter 4 emphasizes, at major transition points from being a student to being a lawyer where the student has engaged in authentic professional experiences (for example, immediately after summer internships or clerkships, and in conjunction with externships, clinics, lawyering

---

[34] *See* William Henderson, *A Blueprint for Change*, 40 PEPP. L. REV. 461, 505 (2013).
[35] *See* discussion of Principle 3 in Chapter 4.

skills courses, and simulation courses). Doctrinal/podium faculty may not feel fluent in such matters, but it is especially important that students hear their voices speaking to the importance of the law school's professional development and formation initiatives. Even when a faculty member does not personally focus on formation-oriented competencies in a course, the professor can still endorse their significance and underscore how those competencies are addressed elsewhere in the school's academic program. Such "cross-selling," as we have called it, is quite easy, especially if faculty are provided talking points.

Principle 5 in Chapter 4 emphasizes coaching as the most effective curriculum to foster each student's guided reflection and guided self-assessment, in major part because it is individualized to each student's stage of development. Coaching is a particularly important strategy for Generation Z, the cohort group born after 1995, now applying to and enrolled in law school. Empirical data indicate that Generation Z prefers timely and frequent feedback that is future oriented, and not just an assessment of past performance. They want personal contact with managers and team members, and they are high on self-directed learning.[36] They prefer and respond best to coaching when the coach and coachee both play an active role in the developmental process.[37] A law school that leads in offering a curriculum of continuous coaching will be very attractive to Generation Z applicants and students.

Principle 6 in Chapter 4 emphasizes the importance of authentic experiences and communities of practice in the growth process from being a student to being a lawyer. The law school should do all it can to create communities of practice between the students and the school's alumni and supportive practitioners, thereby affirming the importance of the school's efforts to connect the students' goals with client, legal employer, and legal system needs. Although senior lawyers and judges may be rightly celebrated, they may be many developmental stages removed from the student. Choose graduates and practitioners closer to the students in age and experience. Students will be able to more easily visualize the steps immediately ahead of them in professional growth.

---

[36] *See* Bharat Chillakuri, *Understanding Generation Z Expectations for Effective Onboarding*, 33 J. ORGAN. CHANGE 1277, 1285–89 (No. 7, 2020).

[37] *See* Elizabeth Deluliis & Emily Saylor, *Bridging the Gap: Three Strategies to Optimize Professional Relationships with Generation Y and Z*, 9 OPEN J. OF OCCUPATIONAL THERAPY 1, 4 (No. 1, 2021).

5.9 GO WHERE THE LEGAL EMPLOYERS, CLIENTS, AND PROFESSION ARE AND BUILD A BRIDGE DEMONSTRATING THAT THE LAW SCHOOL'S GRADUATES ARE AT A LATER STAGE OF DEVELOPMENT ON THE COMPETENCIES EMPLOYERS, CLIENTS, AND THE PROFESSION NEED

The previous practical suggestion focused on bridging students to PD&F goals with awareness of the personal goals that students have and purposeful, effective communication. We now turn our attention to the law school's communication with legal employers, clients, and the legal profession. The law school can build a bridge to them too, helping them recognize that the law school's graduates are reaching later stages of development on the competencies that employers, clients, and the profession need.

One illustrative – and perhaps less obvious – bridge to legal employers and clients could focus on the fact that legal employers currently are dramatically increasing attention to diversity and to DEI and Belonging initiatives. These initiatives drive at the same PD&F competencies that many law schools are choosing to spotlight. An entrepreneurial law school will educate the employers who hire the school's graduates about both the law school's efforts to foster each student's growth toward later stages of these PD&F goals that employers need and how this broader understanding of the competencies needed to serve clients well (beyond just the standard cognitive competencies and ranking students cognitively) will increase the legal employers' diversity. The law school can provide reliable evidence to the employers of each student's later stage development of these needed competencies.[38] An entrepreneurial law school emphasizing the full range of competencies that legal employers need will give particular emphasis to DEI and Belonging initiatives that help historically underserved students understand the entire range of needed competencies and to create and implement a plan to develop those competencies.

A second illustrative bridge to employers and clients – and the intuitively most obvious bridge – would focus on the competencies that research indicates are needed by employers and clients and ensure that the school's PD&F goals well align with those competencies. Empirical research on the competencies legal employers and clients need is getting stronger each year, and a law school should keep up with it and be conversant in it. Figure 6 earlier in

---

[38] *See* INSTITUTE FOR THE ADVANCEMENT OF THE AMERICAN LEGAL SYSTEM, FOUNDATIONS HIRING GUIDE: CUT THROUGH BIAS, HIRE AND RETAIN THE BEST LAWYERS 9–10 (2021), https://iaals.du.edu/publications/foundations-hiring-guide. A broader understanding of the full array of competencies that clients want will lead to hiring new associates with more diversity. *Id.*

this chapter represents a current synthesis of these empirical data, but there will be improving data. Appendix A to Chapter 1 has the current data. A law school should periodically compare its learning outcomes with the latest empirical data on the competencies needed and revise and adjust the learning outcomes as appropriate.

The most serious present gap between the competencies clients and legal employers need and the learning outcomes being adopted (*see* Table 24) is that few law schools have adopted strong client-service orientation learning outcomes on competencies such as superior client focus, responsiveness to the client, and an exceptional understanding of the client's context/business.[39] It may be that the 13 percent of schools (from Table 24) with a client interviewing or counseling learning outcome will incorporate elements of strong client-service orientation. To the degree possible, a school should use the language of the clients and legal employers in formulating the school's learning outcomes. This will help the students communicate a value proposition to clients and legal employers in a language these stakeholders can understand. A client interviewing and counseling learning outcome, for instance, could be revised to include fostering student growth toward a strong client-service orientation.

Two law schools have taken steps that others might find instructive. The University of Minnesota Law School adopted a learning outcome that graduates will demonstrate "client-oriented legal service, including the ability to: … (ii) listen to and engage with clients to identify client objectives and interests, and … (iv) counsel clients by assessing, developing, and evaluating creative options to meet client goals."[40] Villanova's Charles Widger School of Law adopted a strong learning outcome emphasizing understanding of the client's context/business and an entrepreneurial mindset to serve clients and legal employers in changing markets.[41] Villanova's Learning Outcome 8 provides the following:

> Graduates will understand the importance for their career development of embracing an entrepreneurial perspective and cultivating the ability to manage and develop client and professional relations.
>
> 1. Graduates will possess competency in professional networking.

[39] *See* Neil Hamilton, *The Gap Between the Foundational Competencies Clients and Legal Employers Need and the Learning Outcomes Law Schools Are Adopting*, 90 UMKC LAW REV. (2021).

[40] University of Minnesota Law School, *Learning Outcomes for the JD Program* (May 5, 2016), https://www.law.umn.edu/sites/law.umn.edu/files/learning_outcomes_as_approved_by_faculty_5.5.16.pdf.

[41] *See* https://www1.villanova.edu/villanova/law/academics/learningoutcomes.html.

2. Graduates will possess basic fluency in business concepts and termin-
   ology used in the operation of diverse legal practices, including law firms,
   legal departments, and legal service organizations.
3. Graduates will demonstrate an understanding of business and financial
   considerations that affect (i) a client's selection of a legal service provider
   and (ii) a legal service provider's business and delivery model.
4. Graduates will recognize that new laws and technologies, as well as
   persistent problems and unmet needs, present opportunities for lawyers
   in the public, private, and non-profit sectors to harness their training and
   experience to forge new structures, organizations, products, services, and
   solutions.

Empirical data on how new lawyers most often "fail" as associates would be
helpful to law schools that wish to formulate learning outcomes reflecting
client and legal employer needs. Little such data currently are available. As an
initial step to address that lack of data, one of the coauthors, Professor
Hamilton, interviewed ten experienced attorneys at medium to larger firms
in Minnesota during the summer of 2019, asking what are the major reasons
that associates fail to progress in the firm. The lawyers all mentioned a version
of two major reasons:

1. *In the initial years as an associate, a failure to understand and internalize that the experienced lawyers giving the associate work are in effect
   "the internal clients."* Some associates continue to act like a student,
   doing the assigned work well, but not growing: (1) to internalize
   superior client focus/responsiveness to client (the internal client giving
   the work); (2) an exceptional understanding of the client's context and
   business (the internal client's context and business); and (3) an entrepreneurial mindset to serve the internal client in changing markets
   including an emphasis on greater efficiency in producing legal
   services.[42]
2. *In the later years as an associate, a failure to demonstrate the same
   competencies with respect to external clients.* Of particular significance
   is a more senior associate's failure to be proactive in creating and implementing a plan of client development using these client service orientation and entrepreneurial mindset foundational competencies.

---

[42] Two chapters in ROADMAP: THE LAW STUDENT'S GUIDE TO MEANINGFUL
EMPLOYMENT emphasize that in the early years, the junior lawyer should demonstrate
these gap skills in providing help to experienced lawyers providing the work. *See* Benjamin
Carpenter, *Commitment to the Employing Organization*, in ROADMAP, *supra* note 17, at
134–42; Greg Stephens, *Dedication and Responsiveness to Clients, id.* at 109–12.

TABLE 25 *The thirteen most helpful hiring criteria for employers hiring students for postgraduation employment*

Hiring Criteria	Percentage of Respondents Answering "Somewhat Helpful" or "Very Helpful"
Legal employment	88.3%
Recommendations from practitioners or judges	81.9%
Legal externship	81.6%
Other experiential education	79.4%
Life experience between college and law school	78.3%
Participation in law school clinic	77.3%
Law school courses in a particular specialty	70.3%
Recommendations from professors	63.3%
Class rank	62.5%
Law school attended	61.1%
Extracurricular activities	58.7%
Ties to a particular geographic location	54.3%
Law review experience	51.2%

Susan Manch, recently retired chief talent officer at Winston and Strawn (a firm with approximately 1,000 lawyers) recently outlined her similar experience on why associates fail. The chief reasons she cites for an associate's failure are that the associate is (1) not client focused, (2) not entrepreneurial, (3) lacks commitment to grow, (4) does not add value, and (5) focuses solely on hours.[43]

Entrepreneurial law schools will build a bridge proactively to connect with legal employers whom their graduates serve and signal the law school's emphasis on the full range of competencies the employers need. The school also will provide employers with good evidence that its graduates are at a later stage of development on the needed competencies. Historically law schools have not provided strong evidence that an employer can rely upon to indicate that a student is at a later stage of development on the full range of competencies beyond the standard technical competencies of legal knowledge, legal analysis, legal research and legal writing. Note that for many of these additional competencies, practical experience observed by an experienced practicing supervisor has the most influence. The Institute for the Advancement of the American Legal System's 2016 study (with responses from 24,000 lawyers)

---

[43] Susan Manch, *The Competency Continuum: Aligning Law School Education with Law Firm Needs*, at the Professional Development Institute, Dec. 6, 2019 (copy on file with the authors).

noted early in Appendix A to Chapter 1 asked respondents what criteria were most helpful in the decision to hire an attorney. Table 25 has the thirteen most helpful criteria.[44]

While the IAALS survey found that all the criteria were helpful in making a hiring decision, the six most helpful were all related to practical experience where an experienced supervisor has seen the work. In building a bridge to employers, entrepreneurial law schools can ask employers their graduates serve about the most important competencies they need in new lawyers and what evidence the employers would value indicating that a law student was at a later stage of development on the needed competencies. Schools also can work with employers on how to assess new lawyer development of the needed competencies, and also work with them on the use of effective behavioral interviewing strategies.

---

[44] ALLI GERKMAN & LOGAN CORNETT, FOUNDATIONS FOR PRACTICE: HIRING THE WHOLE LAWYER: EXPERIENCE MATTERS 7–8 (2016), https://iaals.du.edu/sites/default/file s/documents/publications/foundations_for_practice_hiring_the_whole_lawyer.pdf.

APPENDIX E

Coaching Guide for a Meeting on Each 1L Student's ROADMAP

Neil Hamilton and Jerome Organ prepared the following guide for use at the University of St. Thomas School of Law (UST Law) for coaching done in conjunction with the ROADMAP curriculum.[1]

I INTRODUCTION

As a ROADMAP coach, you are part of a national movement to foster each student's professional development and formation more holistically. Two major goals of the movement are to help each student grow to later stages of development regarding

1. The student's proactive ownership of continuous professional development toward excellence at the competencies that clients, employers, and the legal system need; and
2. a deep responsibility and service orientation toward others, especially the client.

In other words, each law student has to grow from being a passive student, where the student just does what the professors ask, to become a proactive lawyer owning and planning their own development including an orientation of deep care/service for the client. As a major step to facilitate each student's growth in these ways, each 1L student at UST Law at the start of the second semester has to spend several hours both reading Professor Hamilton's book, ROADMAP: THE LAW STUDENT'S GUIDE TO MEANINGFUL EMPLOYMENT (2d ed. 2018), and creating a written ROADMAP plan to use the student's remaining time in law school most effectively to achieve the student's goals of bar passage and meaningful postgraduation employment.

Current empirical research points toward one-on-one coaching for each student as the most effective curriculum to foster this type of student growth.[2] It also points toward the importance of one-on-one coaching and guided

---

[1]   *See* NEIL W. HAMILTON, ROADMAP: THE LAW STUDENT'S GUIDE TO MEANINGFUL EMPLOYMENT (2d ed. 2018).

[2]   Neil Hamilton, *Mentor/Coach: The Most Effective Curriculum to Foster Each Student's Professional Development and Formation*, 17 U. ST. THOMAS L. J. (forthcoming 2022)(available at http://ssrn.com/abstract=3747309).

reflection at the major transition points in law school, and the period right after first semester grades are out (January/February of the 1L year) is a major transition point where each student needs guided reflection to create a written plan to use the next two and a half years most effectively to reach the student's goal of bar passage and meaningful postgraduation employment. This is a particularly important transition point for the students who did not do as well academically after the first semester as they hoped; they especially need guided reflection about how to gain experience and develop their strengths to realize their goals of bar passage and meaningful postgraduation employment.

Empirical evidence points toward three key foundational competencies for a good coach in this context:

1. Actively listen to understand both where the student is developmentally and what are the student's postgraduation goals as best as the student can discern them at this time;
2. asking powerful open questions to raise the student's awareness and responsibility; and
3. facilitating the student's growth toward the next stage of development regarding the student's proactive ownership of continuous professional development toward excellence at the competencies that clients and employers in the student's area of postgraduation employment interest need, and a deep responsibility and service orientation toward others, especially the client.

Part II of this Coaching Guide discusses the ROADMAP process in which the students are engaged. Part III discusses your coaching goals, and Part IV provides a separate Question Template document of powerful open questions for fostering a meaningful conversation with the student about the student's goals and plans.

II THE ROADMAP PROCESS

The data available indicate both that a major goal for law students is meaningful postgraduate employment and that 50 percent to 60 percent of the 1L and third-semester 2L students are at an early stage of development with respect to taking ownership over their own professional growth to achieve meaningful employment (self-directed learning). At the same time, all law faculties are adopting learning outcomes that include the ABA required minimum competency in "the exercise of proper professional and ethical responsibilities to clients and the legal system."[3] In addition, many faculties are adopting learning outcomes that go substantially beyond the ABA minimum to include fostering each student's moral core/values of responsibility and service to others including the disadvantaged. It makes common sense that a student has to take substantial responsibility in terms of professional development of the necessary skills before the student can do much in terms of responsibility and service to others as a lawyer.

The breakthrough concepts of the ROADMAP curriculum are **to go to each student's shoes** (developmental stage) and to help each student understand the **student's goals** of self-sufficiency/meaningful employment are best realized through the following two faculty learning outcomes:

1. Each student should create and implement a written professional development plan to grow toward excellence at the competencies needed to serve others well (self-directed learning); and

2. Each student should understand and internalize an ethic of responsibility and service to others (this is the subtext message of the student's ROADMAP value proposition and all the chapters about relationships).

Note that the meta-message is that all lawyers should develop the habits of both creating and implementing written professional development plans. Every lawyer should also seek and reflect upon veteran lawyer feedback on both the plans and the internalization of deep responsibilities and service to the client and others.

Figure 7 outlines the ROADMAP process.

Each 1L student will spend a minimum of five hours to draft a ROADMAP template that outlines the student's reflection on the following steps.

Assessment of Yourself

1. What are your strengths?

2. What are the characteristics of past work/service experience where you have found the most meaning and positive energy? Are there particular groups of people whom you have served where you have drawn the most positive energy in helping them? What specific strengths and competencies were you using in this work or service?

---

[3] *Standard 302. Learning Outcomes.*, 2021–2022 *Standards and Rules of Procedure for Approval of Law Schools*, A.B.A. Section of Legal Educ. & Admissions to the Bar.

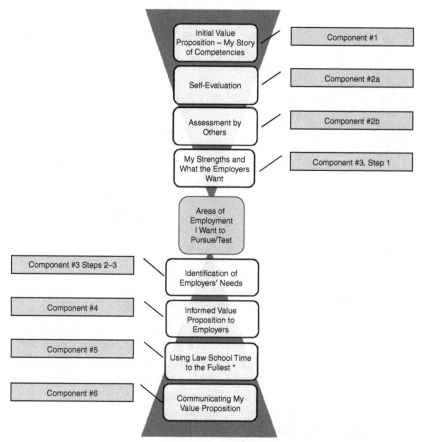

FIGURE 7 The ROADMAP FOR EMPLOYMENT template framework
* To gain experience to test options and to develop competencies (and evidence), and to build networks of trust relationships.

3. How do you self-assess your trustworthiness in the past to help others on important matters? How do others who know your past work/service assess your trustworthiness?

4. Looking at the competencies that clients and legal employers want, how do you self-assess what are your strongest competencies? How do others who know your past work/service assess your strongest competencies?

5. How do your strengths and strongest competencies match up with the competencies that legal employers and clients want?

6. Step back and think creatively about the changing legal market and possible entrepreneurial responses to those changes. Could you

demonstrate some innovative ideas and differentiating competencies to help potential employers and clients to be more successful in this changing legal market?

Assessment of Your Most Promising Options for Employment

7. Can you create a tentative list of the most promising options for employment where you see the best match among your strengths, the characteristics of past work that have given you the most positive energy, and the competencies that legal employers want?
8. What is your value proposition to demonstrate to these potential employers that you can add value beyond the standard technical legal skills to help the employers' clients and the employer itself to be more successful?

Your Professional Development Plan

9. How do you plan to use your remaining time in law school to gain good experience at your most promising options for meaningful employment so that you can confirm or eliminate from (or add to) your list of most promising employment options? What metrics will you create to assess whether you are implementing your plan?
10. How do you plan to use your remaining time in law school, including the curriculum and all the other experiences of law school, most effectively to develop the competencies that support your value proposition? Are you assessing your progress in implementing your plan?
11. What evidence are you collecting to demonstrate to potential employers your development at your differentiating competencies? What evidence do you want to develop going forward?
12. How do you plan to develop long-term relationships based on trust with other lawyers, particularly senior lawyers and judges who can give feedback on your employment plan, help you with experiences to implement it, and help provide evidence that you have developed a competency? Are you assessing your progress in implementing this plan?
13. What is your biggest fear or roadblock holding you back in implementing any of the steps above?

Persuasive Communication

14. How will you most effectively communicate your value to specific potential employers on your list of most promising employment options? Have you worked with the Career and Professional Development office to develop an effective communication and interviewing plan?

III COACHING GOALS

The main coaching goal is to help each student understand the importance of **proactively** creating and implementing a professional development plan to grow toward excellence at the competencies needed to serve clients well, and to seek feedback on the plan from veterans, both now and over a career. This is called the "competency of self-directed learning" in the literature.[4] A second principal coaching goal is to help each student understand that they will succeed at the goal of meaningful employment and career success through an ethic of deep responsibility and service to the client and others.

Note that while self-directed learning is a critical competency for each law student and new lawyer, as emphasized earlier, a surprising 50 percent to 60 percent of the 1L and third-semester 2L law students are at an earlier stage of this competency than where they should be in terms of both their own self-interest and the interests of their law schools and the profession itself.

You can see that Steps 1–6 of the ROADMAP ask the student to identify the student's strengths in the context of the competencies that legal employers and clients want. Each student has a narrative or story of experiences prior to law school that helped the student develop strengths and competencies on which the student can build. Help the student understand that they are building on an existing narrative of strengths.

---

[4]   Malcolm Knowles defined self-directed learning as "a process by which individuals take the initiative, with or without the assistance of others, in diagnosing their learning needs, formulating learning goals, identifying the human and material resources for learning, choosing and implementing appropriate learning strategies, and evaluating learning outcomes." MALCOLM KNOWLES, SELF-DIRECTED LEARNING: A GUIDE FOR LEARNERS AND TEACHERS 18 (1975). Legal educators, legal employers and the profession itself want each law student and new lawyer to take ownership over their own self-directed learning so that they continually improve over a career toward excellence at all the competencies needed to serve clients and others well. This is highly beneficial to the law student also.

Note that some students may feel that they don't know enough to respond to Step 7 with a list of most promising employment options. Please stress that the student needs experience to test whether employment options are or are not a good fit so it is better to identify options and start exploring them. Moreover, a veteran lawyer can help a student far more if the student has a plan with specific options to explore rather than having no idea what the student wants to do with their law degree. The idea is that this is a work in progress; the student will be revising their list of "top three employment options" as they gain experience.

Step 8 of the ROADMAP asks the student to articulate a value proposition. Ask the student why an employer included in one of their top employment options should hire the student instead of other candidates. What specific competencies differentiate this student from their peers? We want to help students begin to be able to articulate how they add value and how they can differentiate themselves.

Steps 9 and 10 focus on how to use the student's remaining two and a half years in law school both to gain good experience at one or more of the student's top three employment options and to develop toward later stages of the differentiating competencies that the student is emphasizing. The accompanying guide provides a framework for talking through this "planning" process with students.

Step 11 asks the student to begin thinking about how the student can develop relationships with faculty or lawyers who can ultimately be in a position to provide recommendations. This is evidence of a student's later stage development of a competency that the student is emphasizing. Note that many students do not focus on having strong evidence to back up the student's value proposition of differentiating competencies. See the assignment at the end of this Appendix where the coach asks the student to write down the evidence that the student has concerning a later stage of development at the student's value proposition. Talk through with the student the importance of having at least two professors and two practicing lawyers or judges who have good evidence of the competencies that the student is emphasizing.

Step 12 of the ROADMAP asks the student to create a networking plan that helps the student build trust relationships that will enable the student to gain experience and build the student's competencies.

Step 13 asks the student to reflect on the major roadblocks or fears that are holding the student back with respect to any of the earlier steps.

Step 14 of the ROADMAP directs students to take advantage of the resources available in the Career and Professional Development office to assist the student in their job search process.

IV SUGGESTED POWERFUL OPEN QUESTIONS FOR THE MEETING
WITH THE STUDENT

Begin by talking briefly about how you wish you had help of this kind during law school to create a professional development plan with feedback from veteran lawyers. Then begin the process of talking with the student about their experiences and where they would like to be upon graduation. This Question Template is fairly thorough. It is not imperative that you ask *every* question or get to every single topic. We know the conversation is only going to be 30 minutes to 45 minutes generally. Rather, we want you to find the major areas of need/interest for each student and cover a range of the things the student needs to be thinking about to get from where they are to where they want to be. Phrased differently, we are looking for you to be a new voice – a trusted and experienced voice – who can both encourage the student *and* press them toward articulating and actively pursuing steps on a career path.

1. **Drawing on Steps 1–6**, ask the student to share both strengths and earlier experiences in which serving others has had the most energizing aspect or a life-giving quality. A good way to break the ice at the beginning is just to ask the student about both what their parents and family members do for a living, and what the student's best employment experiences have been. Listen carefully for natural networks and strong competencies that the student can build upon. What are the student's existing references? What will they say about the student's strengths?

2. **Connecting with Step 7**, ask the student to describe the discernment process that led the student to identify their three most promising employment options at this time.

3. **It is helpful here to make sure you have an understanding of the student's academic situation and their sense of how to make progress on the law school learning curve. Ask, "How did your first semester go in terms of your academic performance?" (What are your grades?)** This is an important question to get answered to understand where someone is situated moving forward. For students who did not have a good first semester, that experience can be demoralizing. Grades will not be their "doorway" into opportunity – they will have to develop competencies and networks to create opportunities. They also will need to consider an academic program (see 5 in this list) geared toward preparing them to pass the bar exam. That is the key hurdle for them in terms of creating professional opportunities.

4. **Building on Step 8**, ask the student why an employer included in one of their top employment options should hire the student instead of other candidates? Ask, "What value do you think you can bring to an employer to help the employer and its clients be successful beyond just technical legal skills? What specific competencies differentiate you from your peers?"

5. **Focusing on Steps 9 and 10**, explore with the student what **the student's plans are for using the remaining two and a half years** in law school both to gain good experience at the student's top three employment options and to develop toward later stages of the differentiating competencies that the student is emphasizing. Ask the student to outline how they intend to achieve the student's goals over the next five semesters by using

   a. Summer and part-time work experiences;
   b. volunteer activities;
   c. the Mentor Externship Program;
   d. the curriculum (skills courses, doctrinal subjects of interest, clinical experiences, externships); and
   e. co-curricular activities.

   Questions worth talking through with the student might include the following:

   a. **What are your thoughts on this coming summer?** Broadly speaking, the summer provides opportunities for part-time or full-time work, opportunities to volunteer, and opportunities to take summer classes in lieu of or in addition to work or volunteer opportunities. Have you thought about when you might want to get part-time work experience in an area of interest to you? Are you watching for opportunities in the online resources of your Career Services Office?

   b. **How are you doing on hours of public service? Have you thought much about ways in which some volunteer opportunities might help you explore some of your areas of interest?** By the time they graduate, at some schools, students need to have performed (and logged) hours of public service. It may not need to be pro bono public service. Students should be thinking about volunteer opportunities that align with their areas of interest or that will help them develop and demonstrate competencies.

   c. **What have you learned from your mentor experiences? Have you considered requesting a mentor for next year in one of your interest areas?** It is always useful to "cross-sell" and help students see mentors not only as a professional development opportunity generally but more specifically as relationships that can help them explore and build networks in areas of interest to them.

   d. **Have you given much thought to your courses for next year and the year after?**

      Ask the student to pencil in a four-semester "tentative plan" on the ROADMAP Goals Worksheet. (One benefit of summer school is that it allows the student to take a lighter load some semester in the future that might facilitate more productive part-time work opportunities.)

   e. **Have you thought about extracurricular activities that would help you demonstrate competencies? These can include law journals, moot court, trial team, leadership opportunities in student organizations, student government, etc.**

6. **Connecting Step 7 and Steps 9 and 10 and 11 and 12,** ask the student how the student plans to develop trust relationships with professors and with lawyers in the profession (particularly in areas related to employment options) to help provide evidence to support the student's interest, competencies, and value proposition regarding areas of employment of interest to the student. This segues into the development of a networking plan to be implemented over the coming semesters.

7. **With regard to Step 13,** ask the student to reflect on the major roadblocks or fears that are holding the student back with respect to any of the earlier steps.

8. **Finally, in connection with Step 14,** ask the student specifically whether the student has sought the help of the Career and Professional Development office with respect to how best to communicate the student's experiences, interests, competencies, and value proposition.

9. Note that the biggest hurdle for many students in terms of actually implementing the student's ROADMAP plan is that the student is too busy. A student must create and implement a calendar with specific goals and specific assessment metrics with respect to the student's top employment options and overall differentiating competencies. The assignment that follows may prove useful.

[Ask the student to fill in the blanks on this assignment.]

Visualizing the Evidence You Have That Supports Your Value Proposition to Your Most Promising Postgraduation Employers

Your name: _____

List your most promising type of employer and practice areas for postgraduation employment:

Assume that you have passed the bar examination. In the far-left column in the table that follows, list the two or three competencies that your most promising type of employer needs and where you are at a later stage of development. These are the major themes of your value proposition to these employers. Practice putting your value proposition in the language that employers use. Then in column 2, indicate the evidence from your resume that supports your later stage development of the identified competency. Then in column 3, indicate the evidence that you will bring up in the interview (just a very brief mention of your best story of your development of this competency and your second-best story). Then in column 4, list the references (if possible, references with legal experience) who have actually seen your work using this competency and who will say that you are at a later stage of development on this competency. You can fill this in by hand if you wish and send me a pdf.

Column 1 Two or three competencies = My value proposition	Column 2 Resume evidence	Column 3 Interview evidence	Column 4 Reference evidence
1.			
2.			
3.			

6

The Opportunity to Lead

You have come this far, we believe, because you are interested in improving legal education. You would like to help better prepare students for gratifying careers that serve society well. You hold that "thinking like a lawyer" is an important professional skill, but by no means all that there is to being a lawyer. You think that being a professional calls for the development of a wide range of competencies. You think that being a professional should involve the exploration of the values, guiding principles, and well-being practices foundational to successful legal practice.[1] You seek to understand these competencies, values, and guiding principles better, and to turn the law school's attention to those competencies, values, and principles in new and effective ways. You want change. You are willing to innovate.

The timing has never been better. Like you, generations of lawyers and legal educators have aspired to help students grow to become good, well-rounded, well-grounded, ethical lawyers – indeed, consummate professionals. Only recently, however, have the necessary tools been devised to take law school support of the professional development and professional identity formation of law students to a new level. The tools for a purposeful and effective curricular approach to professional development and formation are at hand.

The preceding pages provide you with a comprehensive framework to proceed with your own work. Theoretically and empirically based, it is

---

[1] At its February 2022 meeting, the ABA House of Delegates adopted revisions to Standard 303 that require each law school "to provide substantial opportunities to students for: . . . . the development of a professional identity." Newly adopted Interpretation 303–5 defines "professional identity" as an exploration of "what it means to be a lawyer and the special obligations lawyers have to their clients and society. The development of professional identity should involve an intentional exploration of the values, guiding principles, and well-being practices considered foundational to successful legal practice." https://www.americanbar.org/content/d am/aba/images/news/2022/02/midyear-hod-resolutions/300.pdf.

a framework that also is practicable. Follow the framework, and you will be setting clear goals that really matter – PD&F goals that students need to achieve success. Follow the framework, and you can purse your goals smartly, efficiently, and confidently. Over time, in gradual steps, you will realize your goals.

No one can do it all alone. Every page of this book has been premised on the crucial fact that most of a law school's stakeholders have an interest in successful student progression toward the four PD&F goals we have detailed. Not everyone will be inclined to participate in the effort, but almost all stand to see their own interests advanced – although they may not yet realize it. As we have detailed, the four PD&F goals reflect and serve the values and objectives of applicants, most faculty, staff and administrators, enrolled students, legal employers and clients, and the profession itself. Fostering each student's growth toward later stages of development on any of the four PD&F goals is going to benefit the dean, associate deans, faculty teaching doctrinal courses, experiential faculty teaching clinics, skills courses and externships, admissions, career services, and academic success professionals.

Where interests converge lies great opportunity. This book has explained how to build bridges that connect a law school's stakeholders in the common cause of advancing student development toward PD&F goals. Build those bridges, and students, faculty, staff, and other stakeholders will increase their engagement and support. Build those bridges, and the natural resistance to change that is found in any institution will lessen. The framework, principles, and practical suggestions we have offered are meant to enable you to visualize and seize opportunities within your own law school. Use them to empower your own efforts to innovate. Use them to help you lead others to join in, each as each can.

As you and your colleagues take up opportunities at your own school, you have resources to tap. Faculty, staff, and administrators who want to foster student growth toward later stages on any of the four PD&F goals need scaffolding support to make their efforts at experimentation as effective, simple, and efficient as possible, and with the highest probabilities of good outcomes.[2] Those who undertake new initiatives also need and deserve a sense that their work is meaningful and recognized. As indicated throughout this book, literature in the field of professional identity formation is valuable and expanding. A growing number of legal educators are focusing on professional

---

[2] Scaffolding provides a guiding structure and successive levels of support in the early stages of learning new skills. Becton Loveless, *Scaffolding in Education*, www.educationcorner.com/scaffolding-education-guide.html.

identity formation and experimenting with ways to advance PD&F goals. Many of those faculty, staff, and administrators are part of an informal but effective national network that can be consulted for assistance of all sorts. Included in that network is the Holloran Center at the University of St. Thomas School of Law, and one of its major near-term objectives is to sustain and grow that network and facilitate the sharing of ideas and experiences.[3] No interested reader should hesitate to contact the Holloran Center through its website to get connected, find help, or share ideas.[4]

The Holloran Center's mission is to provide the scaffolding support that you, your colleagues, and people like you need to foster student development on one or more of the four PD&F goals. The center's plan for scaffolding and recognition includes the following:

1. Ongoing development and improvement of Milestone Models for the PD&F goals that law schools are adopting as learning outcomes;[5]
2. vetting of Milestone Models with legal employers of all types to bring the models into alignment with employer competency models;
3. providing short online education modules along with short readings for faculty, staff, and administrators who want to move their school's curriculum to support any of the four PD&F goals;
4. providing an online training program and certification for coaches, including a simulated coaching meeting with feedback to the coach-in-training;
5. supporting the creation of low-cost effective assessment tools for all four PD&F goals, including a direct measure for each outcome that will meet accreditation requirements for program assessment as well as practicable formative and summative assessments for each PD&F goal;
6. establishing a recognition program (in the fashion of Leadership in Energy and Environmental Design (LEED)-type certification[6]) for

---

[3] The center envisions one of its roles to be "connective tissue" between legal educators who are working on professional development and formation objectives, even though they may be using widely differing terminologies and thus may not see their strong and natural connections to one another.

[4] Go to the center's website. https://www.stthomas.edu/hollorancenter/

[5] The Center's website has Milestone Models on self-directed learning, cross-cultural competency, teamwork, integrity, and honoring commitments. In spring 2022, the Center will include Milestone Models on commitment to pro bono service, active listening, professional communication, grit/resilience, growth mindset, self-awareness, team leadership, and reflection.

[6] LEED is the most widely used green-building rating system in the world. Available for virtually all building types, LEED provides a framework for healthy, highly efficient, and cost-saving green buildings. LEED certification is a globally recognized symbol of sustainability achievement and leadership. https://www.usgbc.org/help/what-leed

schools that are innovative with respect to one or more of the PD&F goals; and

7. facilitating the creation of national learning communities on each of the major PD&F goals.

Legal education has made marked and encouraging movement toward the support of PD&F goals in recent years. Numerous schools have instituted programs and courses to assist students in their formation of a professional identity. Many have declared aspects of PD&F goals to be among the stated learning outcomes of their program of legal education. Conferences, symposia, and colloquia on professional development and formation are frequent, and the topic has become a regular feature of the annual programming of the national groups that support law school faculty, staff, and administrators. An illuminating literature has been developed, both theoretical and empirical, and research is ongoing. Collaborative initiatives are generating Milestone Models. Pedagogies have been identified. Assessments are being devised. The materials and expertise for supporting the development of faculty, staff, and administrators to do solid, purposeful work on behalf of professional development and formation are available.

The movement has the hallmarks of a *movement*, and it invites your participation. As William M. Sullivan, an astute student of American professional education, has observed, there is distance yet to be traveled, "[b]ut if history is a guide, the new focus in legal education on professional identity formation and the creation of core groups of faculty and staff at different schools around the country portend a possible breakthrough moment" with the potential to effect a "catalytic reframing" of legal education.[7]

---

7   William M. Sullivan, *Professional Formation as Social Movement*, 23 Prof. Law 26, 31 (2015).

Index